Advanced Introduction to Evidenc

Elgar Advanced Introductions are stimulating and thoughtful introductions to major fields in the social sciences, business and law, expertly written by the world's leading scholars. Designed to be accessible yet rigorous, they offer concise and lucid surveys of the substantive and policy issues associated with discrete subject areas.

The aims of the series are two-fold: to pinpoint essential principles of a particular field, and to offer insights that stimulate critical thinking. By distilling the vast and often technical corpus of information on the subject into a concise and meaningful form, the books serve as accessible introductions for undergraduate and graduate students coming to the subject for the first time. Importantly, they also develop well-informed, nuanced critiques of the field that will challenge and extend the understanding of advanced students, scholars and policy-makers.

For a full list of titles in the series please see the back of the book. This is also available on https://www.elgaronline.com/ and https://www.advancedintros.com/ for Elgar Advanced Introduction in Law.

Advanced Introduction to

Evidence

RICHARD D. FRIEDMAN
Alene and Allan F. Smith Professor of Law, University of Michigan Law School, USA

Elgar Advanced Introductions

Edward **Elgar**
PUBLISHING

Cheltenham, UK • Northampton, MA, USA

© Richard D. Friedman 2024

All rights reserved. No part of this publication may be reproduced, stored
in a retrieval system or transmitted in any form or by any means, electronic,
mechanical or photocopying, recording, or otherwise without the prior
permission of the publisher.

Published by
Edward Elgar Publishing Limited
The Lypiatts
15 Lansdown Road
Cheltenham
Glos GL50 2JA
UK

Edward Elgar Publishing, Inc.
William Pratt House
9 Dewey Court
Northampton
Massachusetts 01060
USA

A catalogue record for this book
is available from the British Library

Library of Congress Control Number: 2023951411

This book is available electronically on Elgar Advanced Introductions: Law
www.advancedintros.com

MIX
Paper from
responsible sources
FSC® C013056

ISBN 978 1 80220 180 2 (cased)
ISBN 978 1 80220 181 9 (eBook)
ISBN 978 1 80220 182 6 (paperback)

Printed and bound in Great Britain by
TJ Books Limited, Padstow, Cornwall

Contents

Preface

A few years ago, having thought, taught, written, and advocated about evidentiary law for nearly four decades, I thought of writing a book that I would call *A Stroll Through Evidence Law*, the title to reflect not only the informal nature of the approach but also my intention to dictate much of the book while walking. I was delighted, then, when Elgar Publishing invited me to write a book that sounded very similar to the one I contemplated. Having recently crossed the forty-year mark in the Evidence field, I am pleased to be able to present this book, which has several objectives.

I hope to provide a clear and accessible overview that will help anyone – most notably, but not exclusively, law students in an Evidence course – who is interested in gaining a broad perspective on the field.

I also hope to offer some reflective comments that may be of particular interest to judges, practitioners, and scholars.

While focusing on evidentiary law, I hope that some of my thoughts, especially on the philosophically-tinged issues that it raises, will be of interest to non-lawyers.

And, while centering the book on the American law of Evidence, which is what I know best, I hope that most of the discussion will be of interest throughout the common-law world, and even beyond. American evidentiary law is similar in most respects (though hardly all!) to that of other common-law countries, and I will take account of some of the principal differences. I will also very occasionally cast at least sidelong glances at other systems. But I will not attempt to provide a guide to the law in any place other than the United States, and even in the U.S. there are innumerable variations among the many jurisdictions; I could not hope to mention each one even if I were aware of them all.

Most of the book is organized roughly along the lines of the Federal Rules of Evidence (FRE), though it is not arranged in the same order as the Rules. The Rules provide a sensible structure for most of evidentiary law, one that is of course familiar to American lawyers and law students. I hope that this organization, with chapter and subchapter headings referring to particular Rules, will make it easier for them to use without creating difficulties for other readers. I will not attempt to cover all the Rules; this is not an encyclopedia. (Note that I have capitalized the word "Rules" here, because I am referring to particular portions of the Federal Rules of Evidence; I have left the word uncapitalized when referring to a general, traditional or underlying principle, and not worried very much about ambiguous cases.)

I have tried to keep a relatively informal tone (even though in the end I did not dictate any of the book while walking). I've cited relatively few cases and articles, and in recognition of how easy they are to find nowadays and to save clutter, I have not provided full citation forms; I give the name and date of a case, and if no court is indicated it is a decision of the United States Supreme Court. There are no footnotes here (though there is a sprinkling of text boxes); I am aiming for concepts. I have used the first-person singular where it seemed appropriate; some of what I have to offer is black-letter law, but some is my opinion and, though of course I think the latter should eventually become the former, for now you will want to know the difference. And speaking of you, I have also used the second person from time to time, in hopes that some readers will be able to envision themselves putting into practice some of the ideas laid out here.

For the most part, I have used male pronouns for parties to litigation and female pronouns for other actors – lawyers, judges, witnesses, and so forth.

I am grateful to Kurt Wohlers, who did excellent research for me on this book, in unfamiliar territory. Many thanks also to Eve Brensike-Primus, Stacey Rzeszut, Roger Park, and Paul Roberts for reading the entire manuscript, and to Sam Gross for doing the same with very extensive portions. Roger, Paul, and Sam made detailed comments, a generous expenditure of time on their part that has saved me from many errors and improved the book all around. Roger, along with Ed Imwinkelried, David Kaye, Dale Nance, David Sklansky, and Deborah Tuerkheimer, offered numerous helpful suggestions for the Bibliographical Essay. Stacey and then Lauren

Burke have been my assistants during the time I have worked on the book, and have helped in many ways.

I am thrilled to dedicate this book with enormous love to my wife Joanna, who became my life partner early in my scholarly career. I have been, and remain, a lucky man.

Rich Friedman
Ann Arbor, Michigan
December 2023

1   Scope and purpose (FRE 101, 102, 1101)

Sir Rupert Cross, the leading Evidence scholar of mid-twentieth-century Britain, once said, "I am working for the day when my subject is abolished" (or something to that effect). (William Twining, *Rethinking Evidence* (2d ed. 2006), at p. 1) Was he right? Let's take it as a starting point that Evidence law is concerned primarily with determining what evidence may be used by the trier of fact in determining the facts of a dispute. (There are other subjects, as we shall see, such as when evidence on a given proposition need not be presented.) So why would we ever want to limit the information available to the trier?

The answer often given in common-law discourse over the last couple of hundred years is that the jury may overvalue the evidence, giving it too much weight. But for at least two reasons that is not a satisfying answer.

First, the rules of evidence apply to trials generally; Federal Rule of Evidence (FRE) 101 and 1101 give the FRE a very broad scope. This includes civil as well as criminal trials and bench trials as well as jury trials – and in much of the common-law world civil jury trials have largely disappeared.

Second, exclusion of probative evidence is strong medicine. To keep evidence away from a jury on the ground that the jury would overvalue it, it is not enough to predict that the jury would give it excessive weight; we must also predict that the jury would give it *so much* excessive weight that presenting it to the jury would do more harm than good. I won't say never, but I don't think we can usually make that assessment.

Accordingly, I will not rely much in this book on the idea that evidence should be excluded because the trier of facts, jury or not, is likely to overvalue it. So to that extent, I think Sir Rupert was probably right. What is more, over the long term, the law has moved in his direction: A good deal of evidence that previously would have been excluded is now admitted. Nevertheless, there are *other considerations* that in some settings counsel in favor of excluding evidence so that, in the words of FRE 102, a court can proceed "fairly [and] eliminate unjustifiable expense and delay ... to the end of ascertaining the truth and securing a just determination." Among these are:

- Preventing the presentation of *wasteful evidence* that is not worth the time and expense it would consume.
- Encouraging the parties, and other parties similarly situated, to present *better evidence* – generally, evidence that will be more proba-tive and leave less to speculation. With respect to each of these first two factors, the parties' own interests would provide some helpful incentive even absent a constraint imposed on them by the court, but not necessarily an adequate one.
- Preventing *bias* on the part of the trier of fact. This is a different matter from the overvaluation concern. Evidence that will make a juror want to find an accused guilty regardless of whether he committed the crime charged is dangerous.
- Preventing undue intrusion or oppression by the state. In general, the litigation system claims a right to secure every person's evidence. But there are limits.
- Avoiding disincentives for socially useful conduct. People who are in litigation, or in situations that might end in litigation, are often aware that what they do or say might become admissible evidence. And so the law has to take that into account.
- Ensuring that proper procedures, especially for the giving of testi-mony, are followed. This, I will contend, is at the heart of the right to be confronted with adverse witnesses, and underlies what is worth preserving of the rule against hearsay.

So in the end, we can't do away with Evidence law. As this brief summary suggests, it is a complex field involving a welter of often conflicting considerations. And that means that it bears study and is always both interesting and subject to improvement.

2 Relevance and general countervailing considerations (FRE 401–403)

Trials are about stories. Suppose you're prosecuting a robbery case. You need to present the jurors with a story that involves the accused's guilt and persuade them that, virtually to a certainty, that story is a truthful one.

Let's drill down a little deeper. The jurors will come to the courtroom with a good deal of knowledge about the world. You will present them with information about the particular case, and the defense might do the same. At the end of the trial, you will argue to them, in effect, that to account for everything they know about the world and about the case, they must conclude that almost certainly events have reached the present moment by a (metaphorical) path that goes through ACCUSED IS GUILTY rather than by one that goes through ACCUSED IS NOT GUILTY.

Now, if the case reaches the jury, you have the *burden of persuasion*, which means that you must persuade the jury that you have proved guilt to the requisite degree of confidence, "beyond a reasonable doubt" as American courts put it for a criminal case. But before the case reaches the jury, the defense may move to dismiss it on the ground that the evidence is not *sufficient* for the jury to decide that this standard has been met. Phrased another way, the defense might argue that the court should conclude that you have not satisfied your *burden of producing evidence* sufficient to get to the jury. (Note that the judge decides whether the burden of production is met; the jury, if it gets the case, decides whether the burden of persuasion is met.)

So far we've been thinking about the trial as a whole. But evidence must be considered on a more granular level as well. Before we get to the question of whether the evidence as a whole is *sufficient*, the court must consider whether individual items of evidence are *admissible* – that is, whether they may be considered by the jury in determining the facts in dispute.

Most of the law of evidence, at least as that law is conceived in this book, concerns this type of question. Sometimes the court rules on admissibility of a given item of evidence before trial; sometimes it rules as the evidence is offered; and sometimes it tentatively admits the evidence but issues a definitive ruling later.

The first and most basic question that the court must resolve in determining admissibility is *relevance*: Is the evidence relevant to a material factual proposition, or, as FRE 401(b) puts it, one that "is of consequence in determining the action"? If not, then the evidence simply ought not to be admitted; this, as the great 19th-century scholar James Bradley Thayer noted, is "not so much a rule of evidence as a presupposition involved in the very conception of a rational scheme of evidence." (*A Preliminary Treatise on Evidence at the Common Law* 264 (1898)) Rule or presupposition, FRE 402 states it crisply: "Irrelevant evidence is not admissible." What is more, if the evidence *is* relevant, then the first part of FRE 402 says that it is presumptively admissible – admissible unless, as may well be, some other rule of law prescribes otherwise.

So now let's unpack the terms *material* and *relevant*. In determining the set of material factual propositions, we begin with what the law requires for a claim or defense and then work outwards. Robbery is the act of unlawfully taking property from a person by force or threat of force. So it's a material proposition that the accused used force on the asserted victim, and that means that it's also a material proposition that he was armed, and so too that he had recently bought a weapon. Now, evidence is relevant if it makes a material proposition "more or less probable than it would be without the evidence." (FRE 401) Thus, evidence that the accused had said he was going to a gun shop the day before the alleged crime is relevant, because it makes more probable the material proposition that he then bought a weapon.

I need to be careful in speaking of the probability of a proposition; I believe that probability, in the sense that's significant to evidentiary law, is a subjective matter, a person's level of confidence in a given proposition. So when I say evidence **E** makes proposition **P** more probable, that's a shorthand for saying that a juror could reasonably assess **P** as more probable given **E** than absent **E**.

You might say, "But it doesn't prove that he bought a weapon, much less that he was armed the next day or used force or the threat of force. There are all sorts of scenarios that could have played out." The second sentence is clearly true. The first sentence depends on what we mean by *prove*. True, the evidence doesn't prove the material proposition *conclusively*, but that is not important, because we don't need conclusive proof, even in a criminal case; in fact, some philosophers would say that conclusive proof, in the sense of eliminating all doubt whatsoever, is unattainable, and I tend to agree with them. Nor is this piece of evidence *sufficient* to prove the material proposition beyond a reasonable doubt, and maybe it would not even be enough to make that proposition more likely than not. But that does not matter either when we are determining admissibility, because a single piece of evidence need not carry the entire case. As Dean Charles T. McCormick memorably put the point, "A brick is not a wall." (*Handbook of the Law of Evidence* (1954), at p. 317) The entire case is the wall, and each item of evidence is a brick. The wall as a whole needs to be enough to prove the claim to the requisite level of confidence, but each brick needs only to be a useful component of the wall. Intent to go to a gun shop increases the probability that he bought a weapon, and that is enough for relevance.

You might ask, "Does *any* impact on the probability of a material proposition make the evidence relevant?" Virtually any piece of evidence might be deemed to alter the probability of a given proposition to at least a slight degree, and under the binary approach of FRE 401 (evidence is relevant or not) that is enough for relevance. But Rule 403 says that relevant evidence may be excluded if its *probative value* is "substantially outweighed" by one or more of a whole list of factors. So probative value is what ultimately matters. If evidence is *irrelevant*, then we know it has zero probative value and is inadmissible, but if it is relevant we just know that it has *some* probative value. The more the evidence alters the probability of a material proposition, the greater its probative value, and therefore the greater the probability that it will overcome the negative factors listed in Rule 403. The explicit reference to "outweigh[ing]" makes clear that the judge is expected to balance competing considerations.

The balancing power expressed by Rule 403, which trial judges have had for just about ever in the common-law system, is incredibly important. It reminds us that, no matter how much we might try to come up with *rules* of Evidence, ultimately the trial court almost always has the power to say, "No, I'm not going to let that in. It would take too much time." Or "It would be too confusing." Or "It would bias the jury." Or "We've heard enough about that already." Or, maybe, just about anything; an appellate court will not frequently reverse a judgment because it thinks the trial judge went overboard in making a determination of this sort.

In some common-law jurisdictions, the power of the judge to reject evidence offered by a criminal defendant on such open-ended discretionary grounds is in serious doubt.

Because Rule 403 determinations are so varied, I will not have much more to say about them here. We will instead examine at length numerous *categorical* rules of exclusion – that is, rules meant to cover certain frequently recurring situations with a generally applicable rule of exclusion, which may be based at least in part on the type of considerations that enter into the Rule 403 balance.

But before we leave the general topic of probative value, I do want to mention one tool that is often very helpful in thinking about it. I will use the term *trace evidence* in a broad sense to include any evidence that appears to have resulted from the events at issue. That can include not only physical traces such as blood stains or tire tracks but also statements of eyewitnesses. In assessing the probative value of trace evidence, it is useful to invoke the concept of the *likelihood ratio*. The numerator of the ratio is the probability that *if* the hypothesis being tested – say, the proposition that the defendant is guilty – is true then the evidence in question would arise. And the denominator is the probability that if that hypothesis is *not* true then the evidence would arise. A very high likelihood ratio indicates that the evidence has significant probative value in favor of the hypothesis; if the ratio is very low, that indicates significant probative value *against* the hypothesis; and if the ratio is about one, that indicates that the evidence doesn't have much probative value at all.

So suppose that Dennis's fingerprints were found on a murder weapon, lying close to the victim. His lawyer might argue, "The probability that *if* Dennis committed the murder he would be dumb enough to leave his fingerprints on the weapon is very small." Perhaps, but that argument is incomplete, like one-hand clapping. The argument addresses the numerator of the likelihood ratio but not the denominator. Even if the jurors accept that the numerator is small, if they believe that the denominator is much smaller – that if Dennis did *not* commit the murder it is almost inconceivable that his fingerprints would be on the weapon near the victim's body – they will accord great probative value to the evidence.

That does not necessarily mean that the jury will conclude that Dennis is guilty; that conclusion will depend also on what we may call the *prior probability*, the probability of guilt as assessed on the basis of everything else the jury knows about the world and about the case. All other things being equal, the higher the prior probability of guilt, then the higher the *posterior probability* of guilt – that is, the probability as assessed after taking the new evidence into account. And for a given prior probability, the higher the likelihood ratio, the higher the posterior probability.

> According to *Bayes' Theorem*, the posterior odds of a proposition equal the prior odds times the likelihood ratio. (The odds of a proposition equal the probability that it is true divided by the probability that it is not true.) So if the prior odds that Defendant handled explosives are 2:1, and a given test has a likelihood ratio of 10:1, the posterior odds are 20:1.

Here's a quick summary of some the main points discussed in this chapter: If an item of evidence isn't relevant to a material proposition, it isn't admissible. If it is relevant – or more precisely, if it has substantial probative value – then it will be admissible unless there's good reason not to admit it. To say that the item is not in itself sufficient to prove the proposition is not a reason for exclusion. But the trial judge can exclude it if in her judgment the probative value is outweighed by other factors, such as prejudice and waste of time; in assessing probative value, the likelihood ratio is often illuminating. Probative evidence may also fall within a categorical rule of exclusion designed to address recurring situations. We will now turn our attention to such rules. And we'll start with a big one.

3 Confrontation and hearsay: historical background (FRE 801-807)

For more than two centuries, the rule against hearsay has been perhaps the most salient feature of the common law of Evidence. Hearsay law is complex, confusing, and often bizarre. In recent decades, it has been severely weakened in many common-law jurisdictions, especially but not only in civil litigation.

Running alongside the rule against hearsay is a much older principle, one with roots in ancient times, that I will call the confrontation principle. Here is a brief statement of the principle as it has developed in common-law systems: A witness against a party must testify in the presence of and subject to examination by that party, and under oath. This examination must occur at trial unless the witness is unavailable then. In some circumstances, however, the party may forfeit the right of confrontation by wrongful conduct that renders the witness unable to testify subject to confrontation.

> The ordinary requirement of examination at trial is closely akin to what Paul Roberts calls "the principle of orality." *Witness Testimony and the Principle of Orality*, in Paul Roberts & Adrian Zuckerman, *Criminal Evidence* (3d ed. 2022), at p. 311.

In criminal prosecutions in the United States, the principle is reflected in the Confrontation Clause of the Sixth Amendment to the Constitution, which provides that "[i]n all criminal prosecutions, the accused shall enjoy the right ... to be confronted with the witnesses against him." And Article 6(3)(d) of the European Convention on Human Rights (ECHR) runs along similar lines, though without quite the same breadth or intensity, proclaiming that "[e]veryone charged with a criminal offence" has a right "to examine or have examined the witnesses against him."

I will contend here that most of what is worth saving in the rule against hearsay is contained in the confrontation principle (if you disagree, you will not be alone), and in fact that principle is a critical one that should be carefully protected, especially in criminal prosecutions.

Any adjudicative system that seeks to take a rational approach to fact-finding must rely to a substantial extent on the testimony of witnesses. Then, almost inevitably, arises the question of how those witnesses shall give their testimony. There are various possibilities. Witnesses could give their testimony in writing, as happened at times in ancient Greece. Or they could testify in front of government officials but nobody else, as was the traditional procedure in the courts of continental Europe; this was thought to minimize the danger of intimidation of witnesses. But the ancient Hebrews and Romans followed another method, expressed by the frequently used locution that a witness accusing a person testified *face to face* with him. And from an early time, the English took pride in the fact that witnesses testified not only face to face with the party against whom they were testifying, subject to adverse examination, but also, except in exigent circumstances, in open court.

So that, in a nutshell, is the confrontation principle, a basic rule of *procedure* requiring that trial witnesses should testify in the presence of the adverse party, subject to cross-examination, in no other way, and if reasonably possible in open court. This principle traveled to America, and after the Revolution began it was enshrined in many of the constitutions of the new states, some of them using the "face to face" formula and others using language similar to the phrasing that was included in the Sixth Amendment in 1791.

> Of course, cross-examination now is usually by counsel, though the accused is present; in some cases, English law prevents the accused personally from questioning the witness.

Notice that in this account of the confrontation principle, I have not referred at all to hearsay. Though courts and commentators occasionally spoke of hearsay, there really was no developed hearsay law as such; that did not begin to occur until the last couple of decades of the 18th century, around the time of adoption of the Confrontation Clause. The confrontation right is not a constitutional law of hearsay; rather, it is a rule about how witnesses are to testify. And it is enforced by excluding testimony that is not taken in the prescribed manner.

But in the last years of the 18th century, as defense lawyers played a more significant role in English criminal trials, the nascent rule against hearsay began playing a larger role, and it crowded out the earlier discussion about bringing witnesses face to face. Any time evidence is presented of a statement made at an earlier time, if that statement is being offered to prove that what it asserted is true, a lawyer on the other side is likely to react by saying, "I can't cross-examine the maker of that statement!" Note that this concern arises whether or not the maker of the earlier statement – we will call that person the *declarant* – was testifying when she made the statement. And so the rule soon crystallized: *Any* out-of-court state-ment, offered to prove the truth of what it asserted, was deemed hearsay and presumptively inadmissible. And that is the modern rule against hearsay, though as soon as we recite it we also have to emphasize that the presumptive inadmissibility is often overcome because there are so many exemptions to the rule.

At first, the rule against hearsay broadened in scope. Indeed, in 1838, in *Wright v. Tatham*, discussed later in this chapter, the House of Lords held that evidence of conduct that did not actually assert the proposition it was offered to prove, but which purportedly reflected the actor's belief in that proposition and so made the proposition more likely, should be treated as hearsay. *Wright* was the high-water mark, however. Any rule excluding all of hearsay, especially in the expanded concept adopted by *Wright*, would keep out an intolerably great amount of evidence. And so began a steady process of chipping away at the rule against hearsay by developing and expanding exceptions to it. This left the rule seeming like more hole than cheese, and made it difficult to perceive any underlying rationale. As compared to the confrontation principle, which is relatively narrow (applying only to testimonial statements) but powerful within its confines, hearsay law is extremely broad but rather readily defeasible.

At the beginning of the 20th century, the great scholar John Henry Wigmore attempted to impose some order on the ungainly hearsay mess by pronouncing that necessity and reliability are the factors leading to recognition of an exception. That rubric still has appeal for some; indeed, in Canada it clearly remains the cornerstone of the analysis of hearsay. (*R. v. Bradshaw* (SCC 2017)) Ultimately, though, it is unconvincing: There is always a need for useful evidence, and very little evidence is truly reliable – even live testimony of an eyewitness, the gold standard against which hearsay is measured, is notoriously unreliable.

> In fact – a theme that will pop up at various points in this book – I believe courts should pretty much stop talking about reliability with respect to evidence. Truly reliable evidence, which I think means evidence with a very high likelihood ratio because it would be extremely unlikely to arise if the proposition at issue were false, is hard to find.

As a result, the confrontation became occluded, and hearsay law began to feel like an unavoidable nuisance; courts and rulemakers had a vague sense that it was important to maintain some sort of rule, but they looked for opportunities to minimize its impact. The Federal Rules of Evidence, which went into effect in 1975, reflected and deepened this trend, incorporating nearly 30 exemptions from the rule against hearsay, or more depending how one counts.

> I use the term exemption here, rather than exception, to include carve-outs from the definition of hearsay as well as provisions that certain categories of hearsay are not excluded by the rule.

The United States Supreme Court laid the ground for a dramatic change in 1965, when it decided in *Pointer v. Texas* that the Confrontation Clause was applicable to the states. Until then, the Clause constrained only federal prosecutions, and that diminished the urgency for maintaining a clear distinction between the demands of the Clause and those of hearsay law: If the Court felt that a given statement should be excluded, there would be essentially no difference whether it invoked the rule against hearsay or the Confrontation Clause. But *Pointer* changed that. The U.S. Supreme Court does not control the hearsay law of the states, so it could not reverse a state judgment of conviction on the ground that the trial court had admitted hearsay it should not have under state law. But given *Pointer*, it *can* reverse on the ground that the state trial court violated the accused's confrontation right. And so it became important to develop a conception of what is required by the Confrontation Clause, as opposed to the hearsay rule.

At first, the Supreme Court did not think particularly seriously about the issue. In *Ohio v. Roberts* (1980) and ensuing cases, it treated the Clause as virtually a constitutionalization of the rule against hearsay, with an emphasis on sorting out supposedly reliable from unreliable evidence: If a statement fit within a "firmly rooted" hearsay exception, it was deemed to satisfy the Clause. But then came the momentous case of *Crawford v. Washington* (2004).

Crawford grew out of a knife fight. Later that day, in the police station, Crawford's wife Sylvia made a formal, recorded statement that was not helpful to Crawford's contention that he had acted in self-defense. Sylvia did not testify at his trial.

An interesting sidelight: The reason Sylvia did not testify at trial was that Crawford himself claimed a spousal privilege preventing her from doing so. The state supreme court held that he did not have to choose between the privilege and his confrontation right, and the U.S. Supreme Court let that holding stand.

The trial court allowed the prosecution to introduce Sylvia's recorded statement. Crawford was convicted, an intermediate appellate court reversed, and the Washington Supreme Court reinstated the conviction; under the *Roberts* regime, this was a close and debatable case.

Which was precisely the problem. The U.S. Supreme Court, in holding that the statement could not be admitted, fundamentally transformed the law of the Confrontation Clause. The Clause is not an attempt to sort out reliable from unreliable evidence, the Court held, but rather a *procedural* rule prohibiting prosecution witnesses from testifying out of court.

Now, the state did not *label* Sylvia's station-house statement as testimony, but that is what it was in substance. If that statement were admissible, then we would have a system in which a witness could testify against an accused by doing what Sylvia did – going to a police station-house and making a statement. Or, for that matter, she could stay at home, write out a statement or record it by other means, and send it in. Comparable testimony would not have been allowed in the 17th century; it is striking that it took a sea change in the law to establish that principle in the 21st century.

So now the key to knowing whether a statement is barred by the Confrontation Clause is to determine whether it is *testimonial* in nature. Though that term is not found in the Clause, the choice to use it was not adventitious: Testifying is what witnesses do. (In many languages, the words for *witness* and for *testimony* have the same root.) Most of the Supreme Court decisions since *Crawford* have been disappointing in elaborating on what statements are testimonial, but the basic framework seems here to stay.

Meanwhile, in England and Wales, and indeed throughout the United Kingdom, without any constraint such as the Confrontation Clause, statutory law has dramatically limited the force of the hearsay rule. Indeed, s. 1 of the Civil Evidence Act 1995 proclaims, "In civil proceedings evidence shall not be excluded on the ground that it is hearsay." And even in criminal cases the impact of the confrontation principle has been severely limited perhaps most notably by s. 116 of the Criminal Justice Act 2003 (CJA 2003), which provides in essence that if a declarant's oral testimony would be admissible but the declarant is unavailable at trial, then the declarant's statement may be admitted. But the European Court of Human Rights, with domain over judicial systems most of which have no rule against hearsay, has developed a basic right of confrontation in criminal cases by implementing Article 6(3)(d) of the ECHR. And so we have what I regard as a supreme irony. Courts in England, where the confrontation principle first reached full development, and which long proclaimed its protection of that principle as one of the chief glories of its judicial system as compared to the continental one, are now sometimes told that they should protect the principle by a court that sits in France.

One consequence of this history is that clear understanding in this area requires recognition, discussion, and analytical separation of two separate doctrinal strands: the confrontation principle and the rule against hearsay. The following five chapters are organized by key confrontation issues, because I believe that facilitates a coherent discussion. A presentation of hearsay law as such almost inevitably devolves into a chaotic jumble of befuddling and seemingly unrelated exemptions. But by examining the matter through the lens of the confrontation principle, I believe that we will see that most of the exemptions in fact come close to conforming to that principle. We would be better off if the confrontation principle were the governing rubric in this realm and the complex structure of hearsay law were dismantled, replaced by a flexible and procedure-oriented approach.

Chapter 4 discusses the fundamental question of what statements should be deemed testimonial. Chapter 5 addresses an issue central to both confrontation and hearsay law: whether the evidence at issue is of a statement offered to prove the truth of a matter it asserted. Chapter 6 analyzes the surprisingly complex topic of prior statements made by a person who testifies live at trial, and Chapter 7 examines the corresponding question of when a prior opportunity to examine a witness who is not available at trial is sufficient. Chapter 8 examines the doctrine of forfeiture. Along the way, we will touch on many exemptions to the rule against hearsay. We will deal with them more directly in the two chapters after this survey of confrontation issues, what have traditionally been known as party admissions in Chapter 9 and others in Chapter 10. Chapter 11 offers some reflections on how the law in this realm might change for the better.

4   What statements are testimonial?

The confrontation principle is about testimony. But it cannot be limited to statements that are made in court, under ordinary judicial procedures. The entire point of the principle, after all, is to *ensure* that testimony is given under those procedures and not in some other way. That is, testimony must be given in the presence of the adverse party, subject to oath and cross-examination, and if reasonably possible at trial – not, say, by talking to the police in the station-house or in the witness's living room. So it is critical to determine when a statement should be deemed testimonial.

Crawford did not attempt to resolve that broad issue, because it recognized that Sylvia's statement was "testimonial under any definition." It did note that the term "applies at a minimum to prior testimony at a preliminary hearing, before a grand jury, or at a former trial; and to police interrogations." And it offered some possible definitions, one of which I think comes close to the mark: "statements that were made under circumstances which would lead an objective witness reasonably to believe that the statement would be available for use at a later trial." At times the Supreme Court has adhered to this approach, but unfortunately it has more often departed from it.

One set of cases involves *fresh accusations* – descriptions of a crime made shortly after its alleged commission. In the typical case, a crime is committed, and shortly afterwards a person, most often the victim, describes the incident to the authorities, most often the police or an emergency operator. In the years before *Crawford*, courts had shown a distressing tendency to admit these statements as *spontaneous declarations*: FRE 803(1) creates a hearsay exception for "[a] statement describing or explaining an event or condition, made while or immediately after the declarant perceived it," and FRE 803(2) creates an overlapping exception for "[a] statement relating to a startling event or condition, made while the declarant was under the stress of excitement that it caused." Bridget McCormack (later

Chief Justice of the Michigan Supreme Court) and I termed this practice "dial-in testimony."

So consider the facts of *Hammon v. Indiana* (2006). Hershel Hammon was accused of striking his wife Amy. She did not testify at trial, and there was no showing that Herschel had improperly induced her not to do so. But in the hours after the alleged incident, Amy did make an oral statement to a police officer in her home, while another officer kept Hershel at bay in another room.

Amy also made a written statement, and that was admitted as well; after *Crawford*, the Indiana Supreme Court recognized that this one was testimonial, but thought its admission was harmless error.

At trial, which was held before *Crawford*, the judge admitted Amy's statement and responded with withering scorn to Hershel's objection, because the practice of admitting such statements had become so ingrained. After *Crawford*, however, eight justices of the U.S. Supreme Court thought that Amy's statement was plainly testimonial and that its admission violated the Confrontation Clause. (The ninth justice, Clarence Thomas, disagreed on the ground that Amy's statement was insufficiently formal to be deemed testimonial – an unusual perspective that I will discuss further later in this chapter.)

I believe that was plainly the right result – though I'm biased, because I represented Hershel in the Supreme Court. But the Supreme Court decided *Hammon* together with another case, *Davis v. Washington*. Like *Hammon*, *Davis* involved a fresh accusation of domestic violence, but in this case it was made to a 911 operator, while the accuser, Michelle McCottry, audibly distressed, was not yet protected by the police, and occurred early in the call, while the accused was apparently still in her home. Here the Court decided 9–0 that the beginning portions of the statement, including an identification of the assailant, were not testimonial. I believe the best argument in favor of this result would rest on the ground (which I nevertheless regard as dubious) that a person in McCottry's position would not likely, in the heat of the moment, contemplate prosecutorial use of the statement. But instead, the majority opinion announced this test:

> Statements are nontestimonial when made in the course of police interrogation under circumstances objectively indicating that the primary purpose of the interrogation is to enable police assistance to meet an ongoing emergency. They are testimonial when the circumstances objectively indicate that there is no such ongoing emergency, and that the primary purpose of the interrogation is to establish or prove past events potentially relevant to later criminal prosecution.

In his separate opinion, Justice Thomas emphasized the ambiguity of this "primary purpose" test. People often act with multiple motives, and it is a hopeless task, and in this context not a useful one, to try to determine which is "primary." In many settings, courts eager not to deprive a jury of probative information have little difficulty characterizing a non-evidentiary purpose as the primary one. Consider, for example, a statement, made by the victim of a violent crime to a medical caregiver, describing the crime. Courts have tended to characterize such statements as primarily made for medical purposes and so held them to be non-testimonial – which of course invites an easy way around confrontation requirements – despite the readily apparent fact that any victim other than a young child making such a statement must recognize that it will likely be used in prosecution of the person accused.

So much, for now, for fresh accusations. Another set of cases has concerned reports issued by forensic laboratories. In the years before *Crawford*, many states had taken advantage of judicial laxity by adopting procedures under which these lab reports – indicating, for example, that a given substance was an illicit drug – could be admitted without the author testifying as a live witness.

Even after *Crawford*, some courts had thought lab reports were admissible notwithstanding *Crawford* because they fit within the hearsay exception for routinely kept records (sometimes referred to as the business-records exception). But hearsay exceptions do not control the confrontation right, and if the routine function that a given type of report supports is prosecution, then the report is plainly testimonial. In England and Wales, CJA 2003, s. 117 reflects this principle by making the business-documents exception presumptively inapplicable to documents prepared for prosecution – but that presumption can be overcome by showing that the author is unavailable within the broad unavailability standards of s. 116(2).

But in *Melendez-Diaz v. Massachusetts* (2009), a majority of the Supreme Court, in an opinion by Justice Antonin Scalia, the author of the majority opinion in *Crawford*, easily reached what should have been an obvious conclusion: that such reports are testimonial. What is more, the opinion did not refer to the "primary purpose" test; instead, it appeared to apply the optimal test, based on what would be the reasonable anticipation of a person in the position of the maker of the statement. And here, it was clear that such a person would anticipate trial use of the statement.

Melendez-Diaz was decided by a bare 5–4 majority. The four dissenters appeared to be motivated largely by fear that the result would lead to massive inefficiencies in prosecuting crime, because analysts would so frequently be pulled from their lab desks to testify in court. Such fears were not justified by the experience of the states that had always followed the rule required by *Melendez-Diaz*; very often, an accused has no desire for a live witness to testify to lab results. Nevertheless, the dissenters persisted, and after failed attempts in each of the next two years, they got a measure of satisfaction in the third, in the fractured decision of *Williams v. Illinois* (2012).

Williams was a cold-hit DNA rape case. That is, a DNA swab had been taken from a rape victim, in Chicago, and sent to a distant lab, in Maryland, for analysis; investigators had no suspects at that time. At trial, nobody from the lab testified live, but the lab's report indicated a DNA profile that an in-court witness testified matched that of Williams, who lived in Chicago. Prosecutors were also able to gather and present some other evidence against Williams, and he was convicted.

You can see the lab's report at http://www-personal.umich.edu/~rdfrdman/CellmarkRpt3.pdf.

A 5–4 majority of the U.S. Supreme Court concluded, without agreeing on the grounds, that the statement was not testimonial, so the Confrontation Clause never came into play. The four dissenters from *Melendez-Diaz* would have concluded that the report was not testimonial because it "was not prepared for the primary purpose of accusing a targeted individual." (567 U.S. at 84 (opinion of Alito, J.)) That was a startling standard; it would render non-testimonial, and so outside the reach of the Confrontation Clause, a statement to or by a police officer describing a crime scene, or for that matter a statement describing the crime itself without indicating who the perpetrator was. (And at least in one view the characterization was not even accurate; the report asserted that a person with a given DNA profile, a conjunction of so many features that it was probably unique among all humans who have ever lived, was the source of the DNA sample.) The foursome also asserted that the primary purpose of the report was not "to create evidence for use at trial" but "to catch a dangerous rapist who was still at large," (*Id.*), a distinction that appears to overlook the virtual inevitability that if the rapist was caught, DNA results would be a critical part of an ensuing prosecution. Five justices rejected the analysis offered by the four.

But Justice Thomas, who had been in the majority in *Melendez-Diaz*, also concluded that the report was not testimonial, on grounds the other justices regarded as idiosyncratic: He believed the report "lacked the requisite 'formality and solemnity' to be considered 'testimonial.'" (567 U.S. at 104 (Thomas, J., concurring in the judgment)) Although it was on letterhead, titled *Report of Laboratory Examination*, addressed to a recipient at the Forensic Science Center in Chicago, signed by two reviewers, bore a case number of that Center, and referred to the "exhibits received" and the disposition of "evidence," that was not enough for Justice Thomas; he emphasized especially that the report was "neither a sworn nor a certified declaration of fact" and that "it was not the product of any sort of formalized dialogue resembling custodial interrogation." (*Id.* at 111)

Not only was Justice Thomas's refusal to find this report sufficiently formal or solemn to be deemed testimonial perplexing, but his emphasis on formality seems misguided. The Confrontation Clause is meant to ensure that testimony is given under suitable formalities. If a statement is testimonial in all other respects – if everybody concerned understands that it will be used as part of a prosecution, and perhaps even desire that result – the fact that it is given informally should not take it out of the reach of the Confrontation Clause. In a concurring opinion in a subsequent case, *Ohio v. Clark* (2015), in which the Court held unsurprisingly that a statement by a three-year-old boy was not testimonial, Justice Thomas appeared to shift his emphasis to a considerable extent from formality to solemnity. The latter term appears to come closer to the mark of what makes a statement testimonial – solemnity in the sense of appreciating the gravity of the consequences of one's statement, that it may be used as evidence in a judicial proceeding and have profound implications for one or more people.

5 Statements offered for their truth (FRE 801(c))

If a statement is offered to prove that what it asserts is true, then it raises a potential problem under the hearsay rule and (if the statement is testimonial) the confrontation right. Thus, suppose Jack is being prosecuted for robbing a liquor store at 3:20 pm on December 29, and the prosecution wants to present evidence that Rebecca later told a police officer, "I saw Jack go into the liquor store at around 3:15 on December 29." That statement (which is testimonial) has probative value *if* it is true, because it makes it more likely that Jack robbed the store shortly afterwards. And so there is a confrontation-hearsay problem.

And the converse is also true: If (or to the extent that) a statement is offered on some ground *other than* to prove that a matter it asserted is true, then it is not hearsay (see FRE 801(c)), and neither, under long-standing principles, does it violate the confrontation right. Suppose, for example, that Defendant is accused of making a fraudulent land sale, and Plaintiff offers his testimony that, at a time when the land was actually a valueless swamp, Defendant told him, "This land is worth $10,000 an acre." Clearly, Plaintiff is not offering the statement to prove the truth of the assertion; on the contrary, Plaintiff contends that the assertion was false. Rather, Plaintiff is offering the statement because it is the communication by which the fraud was perpetrated. There is no hearsay problem.

I will refer throughout this book to *plaintiffs*. In England and Wales, the term now used is *claimant*, and in Scotland it is *pursuer*.

And consider also *Tennessee v. Street* (1985). Street confessed to murder. But he testified at trial that the sheriff had read to him from a confession by another man, Peele, and pressured him to say the same thing. The prosecution was then allowed to read Peele's confession to the jury, and the Supreme Court held that this was permissible – not to prove the truth of Peele's confession but to highlight differences from Street's and so rebut the argument of coercion.

The basic idea is this: For purposes of both the confrontation right and the hearsay rule, there is no problem unless the trier of fact is being asked to rely on the statement as a truthful report of some event or condition. If the statement has sufficient probative value to be admitted on some *other* ground, then ordinarily it can be admitted for that limited purpose without running afoul of either the hearsay rule or the confrontation right.

One way of thinking about this distinction is to note that when we take a person's statement to be a truthful report of an event or condition, we are relying on certain *testimonial capacities*. Put another way, we can conclude that the statement is truthful only if it is not accounted for by certain *failures* of those capacities. Take again the statement about Jack going into the liquor store. How could it happen that the declarant makes the statement even though the asserted fact is not true? Perhaps there was a failure of *perception*; say Jack never went into the liquor store, but the declarant saw someone else go in and thought it was Jack. Or there may have been a failure of *memory*; by the time of the statement, the declarant had come to believe that she had seen Jack go into the store. And if at the time of the statement the declarant doesn't believe she saw Jack go into the store, she may nevertheless say she did; that would be a failure of *sincerity*, simple lying. And finally, there may be a failure of *communication*; maybe the declarant was speaking figuratively, or talking about a different day, or a different store, from the one her audience assumes. So if we want to infer from the statement that it is a truthful report of what we take it to assert, we much discount each of these possibilities, which are sometimes called *hearsay dangers*.

That might be problematic. In some settings, at least, we would be far more comfortable about drawing that inference of truthful reporting if the declarant testified in court, under oath, and subject to cross-examination. If, on the other hand, the making of the statement has significant probative value for some *other* reason – if the making of the statement is itself an event that is of significance to the action – then we do not have these concerns. If, that is, the fact that the statement was made is what we need to know, even if it was the product of one or more failings on the part of the declarant, then we need not peer into the mind of the declarant, and we can prove the making of the statement just as we would prove any other event.

Now note that it is not enough (for a judge, a lawyer, or a student) simply to say "Not offered for the truth," or even, "It's being offered to show that she said it." If the statement is offered for some reason other than the truth of what it asserts, it is important to clarify *what* that reason is; similarly, if it's being offered to prove that the declarant made the statement, it's important to demonstrate what the significance of that fact is, apart from the thought that if she made the statement its substance is more likely true. Here are some possibilities, neither mutually exclusive nor mutually exhaustive. (Most of these statements are not testimonial, and so would not raise a confrontation problem.)

- *The utterance is part of the story being told.* As the example given above indicates, if a party is trying to prove that fraud was committed, then he has to prove *how* it was committed, and that may well have been through a statement. The statement is being offered to prove the perpetration of the fraud, and not the truth of what the statement asserted; in fact, in that particular example, the proponent of the evidence needs to prove, with other evidence, that the statement is *false.*

  Similarly, if Plaintiff is claiming that Defendant accepted an offer of an oral contract, then Defendant's assertion, "I accept", would not be hearsay. That statement has *operative significance* – making it is how Defendant purportedly accepted the contract – and so the Plaintiff has to be able to introduce it. Now notice an oddity of this example: The statement is literally offered to prove the truth of what it asserts – that Defendant accepts the offer. And yet it is not hearsay, because it is not a *report* of something observed by Defendant. The jury is not being asked to rely on the credibility of Defendant in making the statement; if Defendant did indeed make it, that proves what Plaintiff needs.

Even if this statement were analytically hearsay, it, and some of the other statements discussed here, would be removed from the rule against hearsay by the doctrine of party admissions, to be discussed below in Chapter 9. But for expository purposes, right now I'm just examining the question whether these statements are not offered for the truth and so fall outside the basic definition of hearsay.

It is also important to note that some utterances that are part of the story being told are plainly not hearsay because they have no truth value. Suppose Mob Boss says to Underling, "Whack Competitor," and Underling is later tried for murdering Competitor. The command would be admissible to prove how Underling came to want to kill Competitor. It is an imperative, not in fact an assertion, and cannot be either true or false. It raises no hearsay issue. At the same time, we should bear in mind that it is the substance and not the form of an utterance that matters; some utterances may be in the form of commands or questions but have assertions embedded in them. ("Wasn't that clever of you to hide the money in the well?") And some assertions might be figurative or metaphorical, and even contrary to the literal meaning of the words used. ("Nice work," spoken with dripping sarcasm.)

- *The statement is significant because of its impact on its audience.* Sometimes it is important to prove that a person received a communication. That might demonstrate, for example, that a landlord had notice of a dangerous condition, that a husband had reason to harbor feelings of jealousy concerning his wife, or that a murder victim had reason to fear the accused. Proving that such a communication was received raises no hearsay problem.
- *The statement proves the state of mind of the declarant.* A statement might reveal material information about what the declarant knows or believes or feels. "My tenant's stairway is very slippery," "My wife is stepping out on me," and "Bill is a vicious killer" could all be examples; as in the illustrations just above, they might prove, respectively, notice, a reason for jealousy, and a reason for fear. Now, it may be that the fact asserted is also a material proposition, but if the statements are *only* offered to prove the declarant's state of mind, with other evidence offered to prove the underlying fact, there is no hearsay problem. Note that, in contrast to other not-for-truth bases for taking a statement out of the hearsay rule, statements offered to prove the current state of mind of the declarant do raise some hearsay dangers. Suppose, for example, the statement is by Testatrix about Niece, "You're a horrible person," offered to show that Testatrix was unlikely to make her an object of benevolence. There is no danger of failed perception or memory, because the evidence presumably isn't offered to prove Niece's actual merits as a person; even if she is a wonderful human being, what matters is just what Testatrix thought of her. But there are problems of insincerity and of communication; perhaps Testatrix was joking or lying, or perhaps she meant nothing significant by the

apparent insult. Nevertheless, with two of the dangers inapplicable, standard doctrine places this statement on the non-hearsay side of the divide. Suppose next that the statement was "I think you're a horrible person." Now the statement is literally being offered to prove the truth of what Testatrix asserted – that *she thought* Niece was a horrible person. So that means that it is now hearsay. But it would make no sense for the result to depend on whether the statement were prefaced by words such as "I think" or "I believe"; hearsay law, I have said, is often bizarre, but that would be a step too far. So luckily there is a hearsay exception for statements of the declarant's then-current state of mind (FRE 803(3)). To be technically precise, if the evidence proving what Testatrix thought about Niece is "You're a horrible person" then it is non-hearsay, offered to prove state of mind, while if it is "I think you're a horrible person" then it is hearsay but within the exception for statements of state of mind – and nothing depends on the difference!

• *The statement impeaches in-court testimony because it is inconsistent with it.* Suppose that Dewar is on trial in a drug conspiracy case and Willis testifies, to the prosecution's disappointment, "Dewar wasn't at the big meeting." But earlier, Willis had made a statement, "Dewar was at the big meeting." So then the prior statement would be admissible to impeach Willis and her testimony: How much weight can be put on her testimony on that subject or for that matter any other, the prosecutor might ask, if she says one thing at one time and the opposite at another? But note that if the prior statement is admitted only for impeachment, the prosecutor can't rely on it to prove that in fact Dewar was at the meeting. And if Dewar being there is an indispensable part of the case, and the prosecution has no other evidence that he was, then the case should never go to the jury, because the prior statement was admitted only for impeachment. We'll return to this subject later, because FRE 801(d)(1) complicates it considerably.

These are only some of the not-for-the-truth bases on which a proponent might offer a statement, hoping to avoid the hearsay rule and, if the statement is testimonial, the confrontation right. The proponent need not fit the statement within a particular pigeonhole; all that's necessary is to demonstrate that there's *some* basis, other than proving the truth of the statement, on which it has sufficient probative value to warrant admissibility.

Sometimes courts need to be vigilant to ensure that the credibility of prosecutors does not undercut the confrontation right. For example, suppose Confidential Informant tells Detective that she has bought drugs from Accused. That is presumably testimonial, but at Accused's trial the prosecution might offer the statement on the ground that it explains why Detective pursued an investigation of Accused. Some trial courts have allowed this end run. Careful courts have recognized that in most circumstances the prosecution has no real need to explain why the investigation was initiated or pursued in the way it was, certainly not enough to justify the near inevitability that the jury would use the testimonial statement as proof of what it asserted.

> For those who aren't familiar with American football, an end run is a circumvention or an evasion.

So far I have been talking about the question of whether a given statement is offered for the truth of a matter it asserts. A related set of issues is whether the conduct is a statement at all – and whether this matters. Let's discuss *Wright v. Tatham* (1838), which I described earlier as the high-water mark of the reach of hearsay law. This was a will case, and the issue was whether the decedent, Marsden, was mentally competent. His steward Wright, claiming under the will, offered some old letters that were addressed to Marsden and appeared to treat him as a person of ordinary understanding. Ultimately, the House of Lords held that the letters were hearsay on the competence issue. How could that be, given that none of the letters asserted, "You are competent, Marsden"? Well, the letters were offered to prove that the writers believed that Marsden was competent and that this made it more likely that Marsden was in fact competent. We can see that the hearsay dangers of failed perception and memory are present just as much as if the writers had asserted Marsden's competence. If we take the letters on their face, not as sneakily disguised assertions of competence, the specific problem of insincerity and failed communications do not arise, at least not in their usual form, but they are replaced by a broad, whopping problem of ambiguity: Why did the authors write as they did? Were they really communicating in ordinary fashion with a person they thought was mentally competent? Or perhaps, while realizing that he was in fact utterly incompetent, they felt that as a matter of decorum they should treat him as capable of full understanding? Did the neighbor who wrote about a local dispute in fact hope that Wright, the steward, would read the letter and act on it?

In the end, which do you think is more flawed evidence of Marsden's competence – these letters, or a flat-out assertion, "Marsden is competent"? I think it's plainly the former, which makes it easy enough to understand their Lordships' treatment of the letters as hearsay – and the similar treatment given by one of them to a famous hypothetical in which a sea captain inspects a ship and then waves his family to come on board, the evidence later being offered to prove that the ship was seaworthy.

But there's a problem: We'd lose too much good evidence under a rule treating all such conduct as hearsay. Consider how the issue arises in modern form. The police monitor the voicemail of a telephone that they believe is being used for drug deals. (Or it could be prostitution or gambling.) Of the numerous calls intercepted, none of them say, "You are a drug dealer." Instead, they say something like, "I need a dime tab." In the United States, in the last half century or so, such utterances have been treated as non-hearsay; by definition under FRE 801(a), a statement is an assertion or conduct intended as an assertion, and conduct is hearsay only if it is a statement offered to prove the truth of a matter asserted in the statement. In England, the *Wright* rule hung on a while longer. It still had force in *R v. Kearley* (1992), but it was undone by s. 115 of CJA 2003; see *R v. Singh* (2006).

Utterances of the type just discussed are sometimes called implied assertions. I don't think that's a particularly useful term in this context. An implied assertion might be something like thumbs up for "That's good." Here, I prefer the more accurate, though ungainly, *utterances to prove the truth of an apparently implicit belief.*

I think that evidence of this sort ought to be admitted, but we're in an awkward situation in which the definition of hearsay doesn't include evidence that, because it is highly ambiguous, raises the kinds of concerns that the hearsay rule is supposedly meant to address. I think a key to a better understanding in this area is to recognize that evidence of the types involved in *Wright v. Tatham*, the ship captain hypothetical, and the drug order is almost certainly not testimonial in nature; the letter writers, the ship captain, and the drug buyer did not anticipate use of their utterances in litigation. If we recognize that the real concerns regarding hearsay, at least those justifying a strong categorical rule of exclusion, arise only when there is testimonial conduct – which is almost always, and almost by definition, a statement – we would be much better off. Modern law reaches an appropriate result by rejecting the *Wright* rule and treating evidence that was governed by it outside the hearsay rubric, subjecting it instead to the general discretionary standards that apply to most evidence. My modest contention is that we should accord similar treatment in general to non-testimonial conduct, even when it asserts the proposition it is offered to prove.

6 Presence at trial (FRE 801(d))

Suppose a declarant makes a statement and then appears as a witness at trial. If a party offers evidence of the prior statement to prove the truth of what it asserts, that is still hearsay (at least presumptively). Indeed, that is true *even if* the evidence of the prior statement is the testimony of the declarant herself. That is a surprising and perhaps mysterious result. But a real concern underlies it.

Suppose the prior statement of witness Willis was "Dewar was at the meeting," and in her current testimony she asserts the same proposition. Then there isn't much harm done in admitting the prior statement. But, unless the credibility of Willis has been attacked, a matter we shall address shortly, we might wonder why we need the prior statement given that Willis is able to testify in full. This seems to violate a general rule (known by various names) against bolstering the credibility of the witness before it has been attacked.

Now let's focus on the more serious part of the problem. Say Willis testifies live that Dewar was not at the meeting. We know that the prior inconsistent statement can be introduced to impeach Willis. But why can't it also be introduced to prove that Willis was in fact at the meeting? If that conclusion is harmful to Dewar, he can cross-examine Willis on it, right?

Well, not really, or not fully. "Cross-examination presupposes a witness who affirms a thing being examined by a lawyer who would have him deny it, or a witness who denies a thing being examined by a lawyer who would have him affirm it." (*Ruhala v. Roby* (Mich. 1967)) Say Willis testified at trial that Dewar was at the meeting. Defense counsel might explore details: How did Dewar get there? What was he wearing? What did he say? Eventually, counsel might find a contradiction, or an acknowledgment of a fact that makes the initial testimony unlikely to be true. But if Willis's live testimony is that Dewar was *not* at the meeting, and only the prior statement asserted that Dewar was there, then counsel is, as the *Ruhala* court demonstrated in an illuminating discussion, "stymied." If, for example, counsel asks, "How did Dewar get to the meeting," Willis would likely answer, "I'm not saying he was there." Cross-examination at that point is like pushing on a string; with no resistance, it cannot be fully effective. The situation is as if there are two witnesses, one in the courtroom and one who made the prior statement. The first can be questioned, but effectiveness of the questioning is seriously impaired. The second made the damaging statement, but she cannot be cross-examined. Of course, the cross-examiner can emphasize the inconsistency, but that won't necessarily be helpful; the jury might conclude that it resulted from a testimonial failure (such as intimidation) after, rather than before, the prior statement.

So I think there is considerable force to the traditional rule that a prior statement offered to prove its truth is hearsay even if the declarant who made the statement testifies at trial. But, notwithstanding *Ruhala*, by the time the Federal Rules of Evidence were adopted, the reasons for that rule had become occluded. The rulemakers, reflecting unease about prior statements but no firm convictions about them, adopted a compromise view: They retained the shell of the traditional rule, but largely hollowed it out with three significant exemptions – carve-outs of categories of statements that are defined not to be hearsay when the declarant is present as a witness and subject to cross-examination about the statement. In addition, in another part of the FRE, they included an exception for the text of prior recorded recollections of a witness who can no longer recall the matter recorded fully and accurately. Some states, while adopting codifications based on the FRE, have incorporated exemptions that vary from those of the FRE in one direction or another. For simplicity, we will focus principally on the FRE exemptions.

A.   Prior inconsistent statements (FRE 801(d)(1)(A))

California Evidence Code § 1235, adopted in 1965, departed significantly from the common law by excepting all prior inconsistent statements of a witness from the hearsay rule. In England and Wales, CJA 2003, s. 119 effectively reaches the same result. The FRE adopted a rather unusual middle course: A prior inconsistent statement is declared not to be hearsay if it was "given under penalty of perjury at a trial, hearing, or other proceeding or in a deposition." So this provision exempts from the hearsay rule a broad swath of testimonial statements, precisely the type that the confrontation principle suggests should be of most concern. And note that it does *not* require that the prior statement have been subject to an opportunity for cross-examination by the party against whom it is offered. Most significantly, it covers testimony given before a grand jury. The Advisory Committee that drafted the FRE endorsed the view of the California Law Reform Commission that substantive admissibility – that is, admissibility of the prior statement to prove the truth of what it asserts rather than merely for impeachment – provides "protection against the 'turncoat' witness who changes his story on the stand and deprives the party calling him of evidence essential to his case." (Comment, California Evidence Code §1235) That is a remarkable statement. What legitimate need does a prosecutor have for evidentiary law to provide "protection" against a witness who doesn't stick with her story? If the witness does become a "turncoat" – and there is no proof that the adverse party intimidated her – why isn't the proper response to say to the prosecutor, "Tough luck"?

B.   Prior consistent statements (FRE 801(d)(1)(B))

Prior inconsistent statements of a witness are ordinarily admissible to impeach; the big question is when they are, or should, be admitted substantively, to prove the truth of what they assert. How about prior *consistent* statements of a witness?

As I've already indicated, if a prior statement just states the same substance as the present testimony, there isn't much of a problem with confrontation or hearsay, but there appears to be a violation of the rule against bolstering. If the prior statement adds nothing to the present testimony, we don't really need it, until such time as the credibility of the witness has been attacked.

But now let's say that Witness testifies favorably to Plaintiff, and then Defendant points out that Witness has reason to be hostile to him, because he and Witness's sister recently went through a bitter divorce. If Plaintiff can show that before the marriage headed south Witness made a statement to the same effect as the current testimony, that will *rehabilitate* the testimony, by demonstrating that whatever bias Witness has against

Defendant cannot account for her testimony. If the prior statement contains no more substance than the current testimony, it will be routinely admitted, under traditional rules, for rehabilitation; in that setting, it is hard to discern a difference between admitting the statement to rehabilitate and admitting it for the truth of what it asserts, and FRE 801(d)(1)(B) prescribes that it is admissible for the latter purpose as well as the former. The history of the rule is complex and its language unnecessarily confusing, but as it has been amended it says in effect that if the statement is admissible for rehabilitation it will be admissible substantively as well.

When will that be? Consider the facts of *Tome v. United States* (1995). Tome was accused of molesting his daughter, A.T. She testified against him, haltingly and rather vaguely, describing two incidents of abuse. Tome contended that she was biased against him, because she wanted to live with her mother, from whom he was divorced, rather than with him. The trial court allowed the prosecution to introduce evidence that A.T. had made several other statements, describing in detail four incidents of abuse. The trial court admitted these to rehabilitate and, under FRE 801(d)(1)(B), also for the truth of what they asserted. But the Supreme Court reversed. Interpreting Rule 801(d)(1)(B) as it then stood, it held that the Rule can be invoked only when the prior statement is made before the alleged motive arose. And in this case, it did not appear that A.T.'s motivation had changed between the time of the earlier statements and that of her testimony.

As a usual matter, the Court was correct, and we can broaden the point to include any failure of testimonial capacity (such as loss of memory as well as an insincerity-causing bias) that might account for the trial testimony: If the prior statement was made *after* the failure of capacity, then it cannot dispel the possibility that the failure accounted for the in-court testimony. Nevertheless, there are some situations in which it seems a rigid pre-motive requirement is too harsh. In *Tome* itself, A.T.'s prior statements appear to have been so spontaneous that, arguably, they could not have been the product of a four-year-old's plan to concoct a false statement. In other situations, it might be that an improper motive has arisen by the time of the prior statement but has not yet gained much force, so the statement would at least have a partial rehabilitative effect (see *United States v. Mack* (D. Conn. 2016) (stronger, or additional, motive arising after the statement)). Similarly, if the prior statement was made both well after the event and well before the trial, it could not dispel the possibility that a memory failure between the event and the time of the prior statement accounted for the trial testimony, but it could preclude the possibility that a memory failure between the time of the prior statement and trial did so.

Tome illustrates a deeper problem on which the Court did not focus: Sometimes, the prior statement includes substance that the current testimony does not. Recall that A.T. testified at trial to two incidents, and not in much detail; the prior statements gave details about those two incidents and two others. Thus, the prior statements were indeed *consistent* with the current testimony, but they had additional substance, what I sometimes call an overhang. In particular, it would have been essentially impossible to cross-examine A.T. about the two incidents that she appeared not to recall at trial, and there was no other evidence on them. Tome was convicted on, and sentenced for, all four incidents. This is a problem to which all courts should be attentive, and only some are: A rule allowing substantive use for statements that get into evidence on the basis of rehabilitation should not be used as a wedge to allow in substance to which the witness has not testified at trial.

C.   Prior statements of identification (FRE 801(d)(1) (C))

FRE 801(d)(1)(C), which was dropped from the Rules as originally enacted and then added back in after the senator who most vigorously opposed it had retired, excludes from the definition of hearsay a prior statement by the witness identifying a person whom the witness had perceived. A statement of identification can take various forms: it can name the person, or it can be a pointed finger, or it can be confirmation to a police artist that the perpetrator of the crime is a person who resembles the sketch the artist has just completed.

> CJA 2003, s. 120(5) more broadly exempts a prior statement of a witness that "identifies or describes a person, object or place."

The principal justification offered for this provision is that in-court identifications tend to be so suggestive. That is true, though improvement in that respect – for example, a so-called gallery identification, in which the accused is placed somewhere in the gallery rather than in the dock or at a table with his lawyer – is possible, and prior identifications may also be suggestive.

But a more troubling problem with the Rule is that often statements fitting within it are testimonial statements identifying the alleged perpetrator of the crime. Again, if the witness testifies fully consistently with the prior statement, there is no great difficulty. And arguably if the witness remembers everything about the circumstances of the encounter but is just not able to make an identification at the time of trial, not much is lost by introducing the prior statement of identification; cross-examination can burrow into the witness's recollection of the surrounding circumstances, but it cannot do much with the "That's the man!" conclusion. The real difficulty concerns the situation in which the witness has a faulty memory of the incident.

So consider *United States v. Owens* (1988). A prison guard, Foster, was brutally beaten and his memory impaired. During an interval of lucidity, he described the attack to an FBI agent and identified Owens as the perpetrator. But at trial, he acknowledged that he could not remember seeing the assailant, or any of his numerous hospital visitors other than the FBI agent, or whether anyone had suggested that the assailant was Owens. Nevertheless, his prior statement of identification was admitted, Owens was convicted, and the Supreme Court upheld the judgment. For purposes of both the Confrontation Clause and FRE 801(d)(1)(B), a 6–2 majority, per Justice Scalia, thought it sufficient that Foster had taken the witness stand under oath and responded willingly to questions. His memory loss did not appear troublesome to the majority, because showing a defect in memory is often the very aim of cross-examination. The logic there is perplexing; it was clear that at the time of trial Foster had little memory because his head had been bashed in and that this impairment made it virtually impossible to ask him about the assault.

Crawford, also written by Justice Scalia, did not repudiate *Owens*; on the contrary, the Court emphasized that "when the declarant appears for cross-examination at trial, the Confrontation Clause places no constraints at all on the use of his prior testimonial statements," and that therefore "[t]he Clause does not bar admission of a statement so long as the declarant is present at trial to defend or explain it." There is some remaining ambiguity. What happens if the witness makes an identification statement and then has, or at least feigns, a complete memory loss, claiming not to remember the incident or, perhaps, even the making of the statement? Does that constitute "appear[ing] for cross-examination," and being "present at trial to defend or explain" the statement? Remarkably, most but not all (see *Goforth v. State* (Miss. 2011)) of the courts to address this issue have answered in the affirmative. It appears that so long as the witness has a pulse, putting her on the witness stand will suffice to get the prior statement admitted (e.g., *State v. White* (La. 2019)).

This is an unfortunate result. Surely, in many cases, the natural inference is that the witness, having made a damaging testimonial statement, got cold feet and was intimidated from testifying at trial. But all the prosecution needs to do, under decisions like *White*, is put her on the stand, have her claim loss of memory, and introduce the prior statement. That's not ideal evidence from the prosecution's standpoint, but it's often good enough to gain a conviction – and the witness will be effectively insulated from cross-examination. My bottom line is that the courts have yet to grapple with the complexities of prior statements of a witness.

D.   Past recollection recorded (FRE 803(5))

The FRE include one further provision applying to prior statements of a witness. Suppose that after observing a hit-and-run accident, an observer keeps reciting in her head the license plate number of the runaway car, and as soon as she gets home she writes it down. The matter eventually goes to litigation and the observer is called as a witness. By then, she cannot remember the number, but because the number was fresh in her mind when she made the writing, FRE 803(5) allows its text to be read into evidence. Oddly enough, the Rule does not allow the proponent to introduce the document itself; it appears that the Advisory Committee had some qualms about this type of evidence, perhaps recognizing that it was likely to be prepared for litigation. (In England, s. 120(6) of CJA 2003 does not have this limitation.) But the opponent has the option of introducing the document, which allows the jury to examine it; one can imagine, for example, that erasures would reveal uncertainty on the part of the declarant.

The exception operates only if the witness has too little a memory of the event to allow her to testify fully. The rulemakers recognized that, absent this provision, there would be a tendency for witnesses appearing live at trial to testify through prepared written statements. That is in fact how direct testimony is now routinely given in civil litigation in Britain (CPR 32.5; *Guidance on use signed witness statements or affidavits*, https://tinyurl.com/56bu57cw) and even in criminal cases in Scotland (Criminal Procedure (Scotland) Act 1995, s. 260), but that would have been a fundamental change in trial procedure that the FRE Advisory Committee was not prepared to make. The requirement of limited memory, however, means that cross-examination is likely impaired, a factor that the Advisory Committee noted and that explains its decision not to include this provision in Rule 801(d)(1), which requires that the declarant be "subject to cross-examination" concerning the statement. (This factor should perhaps have been persuasive in *United States v. Owens*, discussed above in Section C.) So instead the Committee placed this exception in Rule 803 – which is also a poor fit because that Rule enumerated exceptions that apply "regardless of whether the declarant is available as a witness" and this one requires not only that the declarant be available but that she actually be a witness.

It is important to keep this exception separate in your mind from the doctrine of present recollection refreshed. If a witness has difficulty remembering a matter, either party can try to refresh her memory, often by showing her a document. If that stimulant works, the witness can then testify from present memory – "Ah yes, I remember now ... ." In that case, the refreshing material is not the evidence; rather, the witness's refreshed memory is. Accordingly, there is no limit to what can be used to refresh; anything that will do the trick is acceptable. Thus, while Rule 803(5) requires that the live witness be a person who either made or adopted the prior statement, there is no such requirement for a refresher (see also CJA 2003, s. 139(1)). But while the evidence under Rule 803(5) is the language of the document, if present recollection is refreshed, the evidence is the witness's current testimony, not the refresher; the jury would not see the refresher unless the opponent wants to show that the witness is relying on a cheat sheet.

7 Prior testimony (FRE 804(a), (b)(1))

The common law has long insisted not only that witnesses testify face to face with the adverse party but also that, if reasonably possible, the testimony be given at trial. This ensures that the trier of fact can observe the demeanor of the witness as she testifies – a dubious benefit, perhaps, because people tend to be considerably worse than they think at drawing accurate inferences from demeanor – and also that cross-examination can take into account any information that counsel has received up to the time of trial. But suppose that the witness is *not* available at trial. What then?

It may be that the witness's evidence is lost. If, however, the adverse party had an earlier opportunity to cross-examine – such as at a prior trial of the same case, or in a deposition – then the common-law courts were willing to swallow hard and accept the prior testimony as the best substitute in the circumstances for live testimony. By the middle of the 17th century, there was a sophisticated body of law governing when a person should be deemed unavailable for this purpose and when the opposing party should be deemed to have had an adequate opportunity for examination. This doctrine was not then considered to be an exception to the rule against hearsay, because there was no well-developed hearsay rule at that time. Rather, it was simply part of the law governing how witnesses give testimony, providing a second-best method when trial testimony was not reasonably possible. It remains a part of confrontation doctrine – *Crawford* expressly recognized it – and it is now also well established as a hearsay exception for former, or prior, testimony, expressed in FRE 804(b)(1).

The first question that must be asked in applying the rule is whether the declarant should be deemed unavailable to be a trial witness. FRE 804(a) lists several grounds of unavailability. Death is an obvious one, and ordinarily leaves no room for doubt. Other grounds can be more contentious. For example, illness or infirmity is one ground. But how bad, and how enduring, does the infirmity have to be? If a witness is eight months' pregnant and a few hundred miles away, should she be deemed unavailable? Or should the trial wait until she can comfortably travel in person? Privilege is another ground. If a potential prosecution witness claims a privilege against self-incrimination, is that enough? Most courts think so, though in some circumstances the prosecution could nullify the privilege easily enough, as by granting immunity from use of the statement. One principle is clear: If the proponent prefers introducing the earlier testimony to taking its chances on live testimony, it cannot help itself by rendering the witness unavailable for that purpose. This principle is a counterpart to the doctrine of forfeiture, to be discussed in Chapter 8.

Assuming the witness is unavailable, then the prior testimony can be introduced if the party against whom it was introduced had an opportunity to examine the witness and a motive similar to the one he would have had at trial. If, for example, the witness testified at a prior trial of the same case and then died, that is ordinarily an easy case. It would be equally easy if the prosecution, knowing that one of its witnesses was in poor health, took her deposition before trial in order to preserve her testimony; assuming the accused has an opportunity to attend and examine, then if the witness does die the prosecution can use the deposition. But in some circumstances there is more doubt. For example, some jurisdictions allow criminal defendants to take depositions for discovery purposes as well as to preserve testimony. So if a defendant takes a discovery deposition and the witness then becomes unavailable, should the prosecution be allowed to use the deposition at trial? Courts are divided; my own feeling is decidedly that the answer should be negative, because the purposes for which the defendant takes the two types of deposition, and so too the manner of taking them, are so fundamentally different: In a discovery deposition, the defense is likely to ask open-ended questions designed to get the witness to talk and reveal as much as possible, but at trial or in a preservation deposition, counsel will ask tightly controlled questions to highlight weaknesses in the witness's testimony.

A related issue is whether, assuming a prosecution witness is unavailable to testify at trial, she may do so remotely. The U.S. Supreme Court, in a pre-*Crawford* case, allowed this in limited circumstances with respect to child witnesses, and some courts have done so with adult witnesses. The matter remains unresolved in the post-*Crawford* era. When the Court rejected a proposed rule that would have authorized remote testimony in some cases, Justice Scalia made a striking pronouncement: "Virtual confrontation might be sufficient to protect

virtual constitutional rights," he thundered. "I doubt whether it is sufficient to protect real ones."

Problems of different motivation can also arise in civil litigation. It may
be that in Case 1 a particular issue is of peripheral importance, and a party
has little reason to be concerned about it, but in Case 2 the issue is central;
the party would have a solid argument under FRE 804(b)(1) that the fact
that it had an *opportunity* to examine a witness on that issue in Case 1 is
insufficient if the witness is unavailable in Case 2, because it didn't have
a *similar motive* to do so.

Another issue arises with respect to successor parties. FRE 804(b)(1)
allows the exception to operate if the *predecessor in interest* of a party
in civil litigation had an adequate opportunity and motive to examine
the now-unavailable witness. So, for example, if after a witness testifies
at trial, the verdict is thrown out and both the witness and the plaintiff
die, the witness's testimony could presumably be introduced against the
late plaintiff's estate in the retrial. Similarly, if a corporate party is bought
out between trials, the exception can apply against the new owner. Some
courts have applied the predecessor-in-interest language more loosely
(and almost certainly more loosely than it was originally intended), to
include any other party with a similar interest and adequate motive.
Suppose an expert testifies on behalf of a manufacturer defendant in
a products-liability case brought by Plaintiff 1 and then dies. Can the
manufacturer use the testimony in a similar case brought by Plaintiff
2? Presumably Plaintiff 1 had ample opportunity to cross-examine
and the same motive that Plaintiff 2 would have had. Should that be
enough? Plaintiff 2 will complain, "Why should I be stuck with the rotten
cross-examination conducted by someone I don't even know?" That
could be persuasive – but perhaps the court should ask Plaintiff 2, "What
would you have done differently?" rather than acting on the assumption
that Plaintiff 1's cross-examination must have been materially inadequate.

Note, though, that even courts inclined to give broad scope to the
predecessor-in-interest leeway cannot use it in a criminal case; essentially,
the confrontation right is personal, so no matter how closely aligned are
the interests of Accused 1 and Accused 2, and no matter how good was
Accused 1's cross-examination of Witness, if Witness is not available at

Accused 2's trial, the testimony from Accused 1's trial will not be admissible against Accused 2.

8 Forfeiture and dying declarations (FRE 804(b) (2), (6))

Suppose Defendant learns that Witness has made a statement to the police accusing him of robbery and is planning to testify against him at trial. "Not going to happen," says Defendant, and kills Witness. If the prosecution can prove this, then under traditional principles, now expressed in FRE 804(b)(6), Defendant should be held to have forfeited both the confrontation right and his hearsay objection, and the statement to the police should be admitted against him.

> In England and Wales, there would be no need to demonstrate the accused's responsibility for Witness's unavailability; recall that under s. 116 of CJA 2003 unavailability itself is sufficient for admissibility, if live testimony of the declarant would be admissible. Death is one form of unavailability; fear, which is to be "widely construed," is another.

It is often said that this doctrine is based on the principle that no one should profit from his own wrong, but that is not quite right. In some cases, the forfeiture is not *necessary* to prevent that result; if the Defendant is found guilty of murdering Witness, he will have come out worse off even if the murder helped him escape conviction for robbery. And in some cases the forfeiture is not *sufficient* to prevent that result; if Defendant is instead charged with murder, he might well determine that it is worth intimidating Witness into silence, even if the court would admit the prior statement, because the statement would carry far less weight with the jury than would Witness's live testimony. So I think the properly stated rationale for forfeiture doctrine is this: One should not be able to complain about the predictable consequences of one's own wrongful actions. To my mind, conduct leading to forfeiture – which could include intimidation, kidnapping, and bribery as well as murder – is comparable to that involved in the classic definition of *chutzpah*: the quality displayed by the man who kills both parents and then begs for mercy as an orphan.

Now consider this chain of events, which has arisen with some regularity over the centuries: Defendant wounds Victim mortally. But Victim lingers for a while, and before death she makes a statement to the authorities identifying Defendant as the assailant. It is virtually irresistible to say that Victim's statement should be admitted at Defendant's homicide trial. And courts have not resisted. The rubric most often used is what has come to be known as the dying-declaration exception to the hearsay rule, now expressed in FRE 804(b)(2). The gates of heaven were opening, courts have said, and no one would want to meet her Maker with a lie upon her lips, so if the declarant believes that death is truly imminent, the statement is deemed particularly trustworthy and is admitted. There is ample reason to doubt this reliability-based rationale, even putting aside the heretical thought that one about to die might use the opportunity to even some old scores. A homicide victim is not necessarily in a good position to know who the assailant was. Note, for example, *People v. Taylor* (Mich. Ct. Apps. 2007) (killer shot victim through a window at night). Moreover, if this rationale is the reason why dying declarations are admitted, it is totally at odds with *Crawford*, the heart of which was rejection of a doctrine that attempted to sort out reliable from unreliable evidence; indeed, *Crawford* recognized the inconsistency, suggesting that perhaps dying declarations should be regarded as a "*sui generis*" exception to the general confrontation principles enunciated there by the Court.

I believe that dying declarations should instead be regarded as an instance of forfeiture doctrine. Let's suppose that the court holds a hearing out of the earshot of the jury and concludes that in fact Defendant did kill Victim without justification. Then the reason why Victim was not able to testify at Defendant's trial was that *Defendant murdered her.*

Hold on, you might say. Isn't that precisely the issue the jury is supposed to determine? So isn't the court just begging the question? In fact, I don't think there's a real problem here. Under the approach I'm suggesting, the judge wouldn't be determining guilt of the crime charged as such. Rather, the judge would only be determining a threshold evidentiary question. This, as we shall learn, is ordinary fare, and sometimes (as in conspiracy cases, in determining whether a statement fits within the conspiracy exemption to the hearsay rule) it so happens that the question facing the judge and that facing the jury are the same. But that is not a conceptual or practical problem. Not only are the judge and jury considering the issue for different purposes, but they are considering different bodies of evidence (only admissible evidence for the jury; as indicated by FRE 104(a), see Chapter 17, the judge is not so bound), and under different standards of persuasion (beyond a reasonable doubt for the jury, and probably a more-likely-than-not standard for the judge). And perhaps most importantly, the judge does *not* announce to the jury, "Now I've concluded that Defendant murdered Victim, so I've let Victim's statement in on that basis. But don't take that into account in making your decision." Rather, the judge just admits the evidence.

An old lawyer's riddle: What's the difference between a murder case and an ordinary assault case? Answer in the next box.

Answer: One witness.

For the present, however, my approach appears to be foreclosed by *Giles v. California* (2008). Giles killed his former girlfriend, Avie; he contended that he acted in self-defense. The prosecution sought to introduce a statement Avie made to the police about three weeks before the killing, describing violent acts by Giles. Now, that earlier statement could not be deemed a dying declaration, because Avie clearly was under no immediate apprehension of death when she made it. So instead the state sought its admission under forfeiture doctrine. But the U.S. Supreme Court took a narrow view under which that doctrine applies "only when the defendant engaged in conduct *designed* to prevent the witness from testifying." That Giles killed Avie wrongfully, and that anybody in Giles's situation would realize that doing so would prevent her from testifying against him in what would otherwise be an ordinary assault case, was not enough. The state would also have to prove to the satisfaction of the court that Giles did so *for the purpose of rendering Avie unavailable as a witness* and not for any other purpose, however reprehensible.

Why? Part of the argument was historically based. In the old dying-declaration cases, the Court said, the prosecution had to show that the victim knew she was on the verge of death, but that would have been unnecessary if the prosecution could just as easily have proven that the accused was responsible for the victim's ultimate death. So in the Court's view, the imminence-of-death requirement for dying declarations suggests that forfeiture doctrine must be limited by a purpose requirement.

My own view is that the imminence requirement can just as well be explained as a limitation on what should be recognized as a *mitigation requirement* for forfeiture doctrine. Under such a requirement, though the accused may be the initial cause of the witness's unavailability, the state ought to take what reasonable steps it can to preserve as much of the confrontation right as possible. Thus, just because a victim is dying does not mean her deposition cannot be taken; in fact, in the era of the framing of the Confrontation Clause it was not unusual to take the deposition of a victim who was lying near death. The practice should not be unthinkable today; the authorities certainly show no compunction about taking a formal statement from a dying victim. But at some point, the witness may be so near death that it becomes impractical or inhumane or both to arrange a deposition. An imminence requirement expresses this concern.

In cases of intimidation, a mitigation requirement might call for attempting to take the testimony of the witness subject to cross-examination but without the accused being present.

A second factor motivating the *Giles* majority was what it perceived as the inequity of allowing the confrontation right to be voided without a showing of intent to render the witness unavailable. I'd counter that it's inequitable to *allow* the accused to invoke the confrontation right if he engages in serious criminal conduct that foreseeably renders the witness unavailable to testify, even if that result is not what motivated him.

And finally, the majority was affected by what Justice Souter, concurring, called the "near circularity" of a judge's determination that the accused was responsible for the victim's death being the predicate for admission of evidence leading to a determination of the accused's guilt on charges of causing that death; the majority spoke of such a result as being "repugnant to our constitutional system." I have spoken above about why I don't believe this phenomenon is actually troublesome. (And note that a near circle is very different from a circle!) But beyond that, the Court's decision does not eliminate the phenomenon, though it narrows the circumstances in which it will occur; if the court concludes that the accused killed the declarant for the purpose of rendering her unavailable to testify against him, then forfeiture would still apply.

Giles raises various significant concerns. At a broad level, the decision makes essentially inevitable recognition of a reliability-based dying-declaration exception to the confrontation right, one that does not fit at all in the general framework of *Crawford*.

The decision also means that some cases that ideally would be resolved by applying forfeiture doctrine are instead resolved by inapt narrowing of the confrontation right. A particularly striking example is *Michigan v. Bryant* (2011). Police found a shooting victim, Covington, lying on the ground outside a gas station. He identified Bryant as the shooter, six blocks away and 25 minutes earlier. Though Covington died within hours, he did not appear on the verge of death when he made the statements, so they were not admissible as dying declarations. Had it not been for *Giles*, the statements easily could have been admitted under forfeiture doctrine. But *Giles* foreclosed that resolution, and a majority of the Supreme Court held, rather remarkably, that Covington's statements were made for the primary purpose of resolving an ongoing emergency, even though they identified the shooter to the authorities and there was no danger at the scene and no indication that Bryant was on a rampage. Consider also *United States v. Owens*, discussed above in Chapter 6. Were it not for *Giles*, a case like that could be resolved by forfeiture doctrine, on the basis that Owens rendered Foster unavailable by beating him, rather than by indulging in the fiction that Owens had an adequate opportunity to cross-examine Foster.

I suppose it's clear I'm not a fan of the *Giles* decision. I believe that until the Supreme Court reverses it, the doctrine of the Confrontation Clause will never reach optimal form.

But, having organized the discussion to this point along the lines of that doctrine, a nutshell summary of it as it stands may be useful and comprehensible: A statement is deemed to be testimonial if its primary purpose is to establish or prove past events potentially relevant to later criminal prosecution. If a testimonial statement is offered against an accused to prove the truth of a matter it asserts, then the accused has a right to demand that the witness – the maker of the statement – give the testimony in the presence of the accused, under oath and subject to cross-examination. That confrontation should occur at trial, if reasonably possible, but if not, then previously given testimony may be used, so long as the accused had an adequate opportunity and similar motive to examine the witness. Under

Giles, the right is qualified by two related doctrines: forfeiture doctrine, which in *Giles*'s version applies if the witness is unavailable to testify subject to confrontation because of the wrongful conduct of the accused designed to achieve that result, and the dying-declaration exception.

Along the way in discussing the confrontation right, we've seen that the rule against hearsay applies in general to out-of-court statements offered to prove the truth of what they assert, and we've discussed some of the exemptions to that rule. Now we'll focus on those more directly. And we'll start with the most complex, far-ranging, and important one.

9 Admissions (FRE 801(d)(2))

A.   In general

Anyone who has seen police dramas knows the line, "Anything you say may be used against you." It is virtually always true and it lies at the core of the doctrine that has been traditionally known as *admissions*: If a person makes a statement and later becomes a party to litigation, then the statement may be introduced against him, notwithstanding the rule against hearsay and the confrontation right. (In England and Wales, Police and Criminal Evidence Act (PACE) 1984, s. 76(1) renders confessions presumptively admissible.) The term admissions is somewhat misleading, because to qualify a statement need not acknowledge anything that at that time appears to be unfavorable to the declarant. For example, suppose that Donald is on trial for tax evasion and earlier, to increase his chances of getting a bank loan, he inflated the value of his property. At the time he made the statement, it seemed to favor his interests. But he said it, and it's being offered against him, and that's enough for it to be deemed an admission. Because the term "admissions" does not fit well, the FRE no longer use it. But we shall see that the term now used by the FRE, "[a]n opposing party's statement," is not completely accurate, either, because the doctrine goes well beyond the core case of a statement by a party, whether an individual or an entity, offered against that party. So I will stick with the term *admissions*, in part because of tradition, in part for ease of reference, and in part because some jurisdictions continue to use it. And I will refer to admissions doctrine as an exemption, rather than as an exception to the hearsay rule, because the FRE, for debatable reasons, carve admissions out of the definition of hearsay rather than treating them as an exception to the rule against hearsay.

Before going any further, let's distinguish between the type of admissions we're discussing here, which are sometimes called *evidentiary admissions*, and three other types of statement.

The first category is what are often labeled *judicial admissions*. A judicial admission is a formal acknowledgment, made as part of the litigation and usually by the party's lawyer, that a given proposition is true. It can be made in the pleadings, or in response to a request for admission under rules such as Fed. R. Civ. P. 36, or by a separate stipulation, stated either in writing or orally in open court and perhaps as part of a broader agreement. ("If you agree that those pictures won't be admitted into evidence, I'll stipulate that the victim died of multiple stab wounds.") It treats the proposition as true for purposes of the litigation, so – unless for some reason the court relieves the party from it – no evidence offered to prove the point is necessary or even permitted. By contrast, an evidentiary admission is any statement by, or for some other reason attributed to, a party and offered against that party. It is exempt from the hearsay rule and, as we shall see, some other evidentiary rules as well. And it tends to be powerful evidence; to take the core case, if a party is taking the position in litigation that a proposition is true and at a previous time that party asserted that the proposition was false, that is likely to have considerable persuasive power. But an evidentiary admission *only* has evidentiary value. That is, the party is free to contest it, contending perhaps that he was lying or joking or confused or just plain wrong when he made it, or perhaps that the statement is now being misunderstood.

Second, let's keep straight the difference between admissions and *prior inconsistent statements* of a witness. Those statements may be admitted to impeach a witness and, in some circumstances, to prove the truth of what they assert as well. But the predicate for admitting one is that the witness has testified, and has done so inconsistently with her prior statement. By contrast, for a statement to qualify as an admission it is not necessary that the declarant be a witness, or that it be contrary to anything he has said; it is simply necessary that the statement was made by, or for some other reason is attributed to, the party against whom it is offered.

And finally, there is a hearsay exception for *declarations against interest* (*see* Chapter 10 below). For that to apply, the declarant must be unavailable at the time of trial and the statement must have been against the declarant's interest at the time it was made. Neither of these requirements applies to admissions. It is worth repeating for emphasis: For a statement to be an admission, all that is necessary is that it have been *made by, or otherwise attributed to, the party against whom it is offered.*

The discussion below addresses first the core case, personal admissions, in Section B, then tacit or adoptive admissions in Section C, agency admissions in the civil context in Section D, and finally statements by a conspirator of the party opponent in Section E.

B.   Personal admissions (FRE 801(d)(2)(A))

It is easy enough to see why personal admissions – statements by an individual party, offered against that party – are exempted from the confrontation right and the hearsay rule. The party made a statement and now it is being offered against him; he has no need to be confronted by himself. Of course, he may want to explain the statement away, but in most settings he can take the witness stand to do that. (If he is a criminal defendant, though, there may be a considerable cost in doing so.) What is more, given that it is his opponent who is introducing the statement, it is almost certainly contrary to the position he is now taking in litigation, and that gives the statement particularly strong persuasive power.

Indeed, admissions are exempt not only from the confrontation right and the hearsay rule, but also the rules limiting lay opinion and requiring personal knowledge (see pp. 117–18) and in part, under FRE 1007, from the rule ordinarily requiring originals to prove the contents of a document (see p. 159). So suppose that Plaintiff offers evidence that after he was injured by a piece of scaffolding falling off Defendant's home, Defendant said, "The workers did a really poor job securing that scaffolding." If Defendant's counsel objects that Defendant doesn't know anything about how scaffolding should be secured, wasn't present when this job was done, and didn't take into account alternative explanations, the court's response will probably be something on the order of, "Tough luck. He said it. Deal with it as best you can."

Personal admissions are usually easy to spot – Is it a statement by the party personally? Is it offered against him? – and recognizing that a statement is one can relieve students, lawyers, and judges of considerable difficulty by making it unnecessary to decide whether a statement fits within the basic definition of hearsay and whether it falls within one of the other exemptions.

C. Adoptive and tacit admissions (FRE 801(d)(2) (B))

Sometimes a person receiving a statement might engage in conduct that, without actually repeating the substance of the statement, communicates his belief that the statement is true. That is, he adopts the statement as his own, and if the statement is offered against him it is an *adoptive admission*. For example, if Production Manager writes to Owner, "The quality of our output has been poor lately," and Owner responds, "Agreed!," Production Manager's statement would, if offered against Owner, qualify as an adoptive admission. Sometimes it can be a close question whether the party adopted the statement rather than merely acknowledged receipt; suppose, for example, that Owner's response had been instead, "I hear you."

Between adoption and mere acknowledgment is conduct that, while not actually *communicating* a belief that the statement is true, nevertheless appears to *reflect* that belief. Suppose Owner's response had been to ask, "What do you recommend?" That does not appear to be an attempt to communicate the message, "I agree with what you just said." But it does seem that Owner would be unlikely to have asked that question unless he believed what Production Manager had written. So we can label this a *tacit admission* (or perhaps we should call it an *imputed* one), rather than an adoptive one. Note that FRE 801(d)(2)(B) covers both types, because it refers to a statement that the party against whom it is offered "manifested that it adopted or believed to be true"; adoption is not necessary. Usually there is no practical consequence to the distinction between adoptive and tacit admissions, but lurking here is a theoretical curiosity: If a party only tacitly admits a statement and does not adopt it, then the statement cannot really be considered his own. The "admission," with respect to both tacit and adoptive admissions, is the responsive conduct – which in the case of a tacit admission is not a statement and so does not even fall within the basic definition of hearsay. Before the FRE, some courts recognized that, with respect to both tacit and adoptive admissions, the statement made to the party opponent is only a predicate for the responsive conduct, so it does not place in issue the credibility of the declarant; the opponent could not attack the declarant's credibility and the proponent could not attack it. The FRE seem to override this nuance by speaking of the statement itself, rather than the responsive conduct, as falling within the exemption.

D. Agency admissions (FRE 801(d)(2)(C), (D))

Suppose Celebrity, after being arrested for drunk driving, authorizes Agent to make a statement on the subject. Agent does so, acknowledging that Celebrity had "a few drinks" in the hours before the arrest. If Celebrity is later involved in litigation arising from the incident, Agent's statement can be introduced against him, under traditional principles; Celebrity authorized the statement, and it is treated for purposes of admissions doctrine as if it were Celebrity's own (FRE 801(d)(2)(C)). And if Agent was nowhere near Celebrity during the whole episode? It doesn't matter; remember that the personal knowledge requirement doesn't apply to admissions, and this point is extended to representative admissions as well as personal ones. And what if Celebrity didn't *explicitly* authorize Agent to make a statement about the driving incident? The statement Agent made could still be deemed an agency admission if the court determines that Agent was *implicitly* authorized to make a statement on the subject matter, and such a finding is more likely if a regular part of Agent's duties is speaking on behalf of Celebrity.

Note how agents' statements extend the concept of admissions, to statements of a person who is not the party even though the party-principal never "manifested that it adopted or believed" the statement to be true. Part of the justification for personal admissions is that the party-declarant can probably choose to take the witness stand to explain the statement away. But that is less likely to be true with respect to agency admissions: It may be that by the time of trial the principal and the agent are no longer on good terms.

Agency admissions are especially important with respect to corporate parties, and other entities. By necessity, corporations almost always speak through agents. (If the Board of Directors makes a statement, that might not be considered an agent's statement because the Board embodies the corporation.) Officers and other employees are agents of a corporation, and are often authorized to speak on its behalf.

But suppose Driver, employed by Corporation, hits Pedestrian and makes a statement acknowledging fault. If Pedestrian sues Corporation and offers the statement, Corporation might contend, "We authorized Driver to drive a van. We didn't authorize him to make statements, especially on subjects like this." Under traditional law, that would be a winning argument, but even before the FRE some courts had begun loosening up, and the FRE took a major step in that direction. Under Rule 801(d)(2)(D), a statement "made by the party's agent or employee on a matter within the scope of that relationship and while it existed" qualifies as an admission. So under this Rule, Driver's statement would be an admission of Corporation: The agency relationship existed at the time of the statement (even if Corporation fired Driver shortly after, and even it if it did so for opening his mouth), and driving the van was "a matter within the scope of that relationship." Note that there is no requirement under this Rule that the agent's statement *further the interests* of the principal, and it may well be, as in this example, that the statement is directly contrary to those interests when made. In no sense is this really a statement by the party against whom it is offered; once again, we have drifted away from the core idea of party admissions.

Sometimes it is doubtful whether the statement did concern a matter within the scope of the agency relationship. Consider, for example, *Wilkinson v. Carnival Cruise Lines, Inc.* (11th Cir. 1991). The plaintiff was injured when a sliding door near the pool area of a cruise ship ran over her toes. To demonstrate that the defendant had notice of the problem before the accident, the plaintiff offered evidence of a statement by a cabin steward that the ship had been having problems with the door. But the steward's responsibilities were primarily to clean passenger cabins; he was not even authorized to be in the pool area. One might argue that the steward, who would routinely interact with passengers, was responsible for maintaining good relations with them, so anything having to do with passenger complaints about the shipboard experience was within the scope of the agency relationship. The appellate court, however, held that the subject matter of the statement lay out of the scope of the relationship between the steward and the cruise line, and the plaintiff was out of luck.

E.   Conspirator statements (FRE 801(d)(2)(E))

Now we get to pile fiction on fiction. A conspiracy is essentially a partnership to achieve illicit ends. Partners are deemed each to be agents of the other. So statements by one member of the conspiracy that are made during its course and in furtherance of it are deemed to be party admissions.

Let's note the breathtaking scope of this exemption. Conspiracies can be broad-ranging enterprises with clearly defined hierarchies. But evidentiary law attributes to them an egalitarian, all-for-one-and-one-for-all spirit that could be a model of social cooperativeness. If Mob Boss makes a statement that, while advancing the goals of the conspiracy, implicates Underling, then so far as the hearsay rule is concerned, that statement is admissible against Underling as if it were his own; Boss and Underling are treated as agents of each other. Similarly, if conspirator Boston makes a statement that advances the conspiracy's goals, it can, if relevant, be introduced against conspirator Cleveland, even though the two members are each unaware of the other's participation or even their existence. Moreover, when one joins an ongoing conspiracy, one essentially adopts all the statements that have already been made in its furtherance. So long as the conspiracy was up and running and Boston had already joined when she made her statement, it does not matter that Cleveland was not yet a member, so long as she joins at some point.

Just as the exemption requires that the conspiracy have begun by the time of the statement, it does not apply if by then the conspiracy has ended, by either being abandoned or having achieved its primary goal. So, a recurrent problem: Wife hires Hitman to get rid of Unwanted Husband. At some later point they have a conversation about their arrangement. When does the conspiracy end? When Hitman does the job? When Wife receives life insurance proceeds? When Hitman is paid? Never (on the theory their aim is to avoid detection)?

Note also that, whatever their relationship at the time of the statement, when Declarant-Member's statement is introduced against Accused-Member, the latter almost certainly cannot put the former on the witness stand to try to explain the statement away; even if they are on good terms, Declarant-Member will probably assert her privilege against self-incrimination and refuse to testify.

So we have moved far, far away from any genuine sense of the party's own statement being admitted against him. Nor are conspirators' statements particularly likely to be reliable. As Joseph Levie wrote long ago, "It is no victory for common sense to make a belief that criminals are notorious for their veracity the basis for law." (Joseph Levie, *Hearsay and Conspiracy: A Reexamination of the Co-Conspirators' Exception to the Hearsay Rule,*

52 Mich. L. Rev. 1159, 1166 (1954)) By now you may be wondering, just why *are* these statements routinely admitted?

One significant limitation on the exemption might give a clue. To fit within the exemption, the statement must be made *in furtherance* of the conspiracy; it is not sufficient that it be *on the subject matter* of the conspiracy. In other words, even though the doctrine of conspirator statements is supposedly an application of the principle that governs agency admissions, there is nothing comparable to the extended reach of FRE 801(d)(2)(D). The Advisory Committee that drafted the Federal Rules was almost apologetic about the inconsistency, but, citing Levie, asserted that "the agency theory of conspiracy is at best a fiction and ought not to serve as a basis for admissibility beyond that already established." Note to Rule 801(d)(2)(E). Courts are often very creative in finding that a statement did further the aims of the conspiracy; conspirators engage in all sorts of recruitment, fund-raising, and promotional activities that are advanced by their boasts, recounting of past exploits, and statements of future plans. But there are limits, and courts will not treat a statement by a member of the conspiracy to a known police officer (as opposed to one operating undercover) about what the conspiracy has done as being in furtherance of the conspiracy; on the contrary, such a statement essentially blows the conspiracy apart. Notice that such a statement is clearly testimonial.

So here is my take on the exemption for conspirators' statements, which requires a rather heretical premise: Let's suppose that most hearsay is actually pretty useful evidence if live testimony of the declarant would be. It is far from perfect, of course, but it is usually more probative than prejudicial. So then the real question is not whether a given type of hearsay statement is such good evidence that it ought to fit within an exemption to an exclusionary rule and be admitted. Rather, the question is whether a given type of statement is so troublesome in some respect that it ought to be excluded. And the doctrine of conspirator exemptions marks out one particular border that ought to be guarded carefully: Statements that further the conspiracy, as the members go about their mundane conspiratorial business, are not testimonial and ordinarily are good evidence. But statements to known authorities describing past criminal activity do *not* further the conspiracy and are clearly testimonial. They should not be admitted against a person other than the declarant, whether or not the two have previously been confederates. This is a conclusion that the

Twelve Judges of the King's Bench made clear as early as 1662, in the *Case of Thomas Tong*, and it should be obvious, but later courts (*see, e.g., Lilly v. Virginia* (1999)) have sometimes lost sight of it. Here, as in many other contexts, I believe that hearsay doctrine implicitly, and largely unknowingly, reflects the confrontation principle (see Chapter 10 below).

The predicates for a statement to fit within the exemption for conspirators' statements, we have seen, are that the statement was made during and in furtherance of a conspiracy of which the declarant was a member at the time of the statement and the party opponent was a member then or later. The exemption is often invoked in cases in which one or more of the substantive charges is a conspiracy crime, based on the same conspiracy that assertedly supports the hearsay exemption. That raises what might *appear* to be a perplexing set of problems. Most broadly, the jury will have to determine whether the accused committed the conspiracy crime, and in the course of the trial the prosecution asks the court to admit a statement on the basis that the accused was in fact a member of the conspiracy. But there is no real problem here. The court has to decide an evidentiary issue and the jury has to decide guilt. Those are separate functions, and the fact that they each depend on some of the same factual findings is neither here nor there. (It's a shame the *Giles* Court didn't take note; see Chapter 8 above.)

The more pointed issue is that, if the statement asserts that the accused is a member of the conspiracy, the court, in determining the predicates for admissibility, will be tempted to rely on the statement itself as proof of what it asserts. Traditionally, this reliance was not allowed. The rule was often expressed as one against "bootstrapping" – that is, the evidence was not allowed to lift itself into evidence "by its own bootstraps." Operationally, the rule meant that, in determining whether the predicates for the exemption existed, the trial court was limited to evidence independent of the statement itself. But in *Bourjaily v. United States* (1987), the Supreme Court held that this rule did not survive passage of the FRE. And that seems the right decision: FRE 104 provides that in deciding a preliminary question bearing on whether evidence is admissible, "the court is not bound by evidence rules, except those on privilege." In deciding whether the predicates are true, the court can consider any non-privileged piece of evidence at all – and that includes the statement being offered. Once again, the difference in functions of the court and of the jury, one deciding the evidentiary issue and the other deciding guilt or innocence, is crucial.

And finally, there is a substantial irony: If conspiracy is charged, often there is no real need for the court to determine whether the exemption applies. If in fact the statement furthered the aims of that conspiracy, then it may well be admissible for that very purpose, to prove how the alleged conspiracy that lies at the heart of the case operated.

10 Other hearsay exemptions (FRE 803, 804(b)(3), 807)

The above chapters have discussed in detail two large sets of carve-outs from the definition of hearsay, under the FRE rubric – the exemptions for certain prior statements of a witness and for party admissions. Along the way, while most of the discussion has been organized according to confrontation principles, we've explored rather fully the exceptions for forfeiture and dying declarations and for prior testimony. This chapter will discuss some significant exceptions that so far we have just touched on or not discussed at all.

The hearsay exceptions can feel like a jumble, a disassociated grab-bag of ideas pointing in numerous directions. But there is an overall theme to the discussion below: I believe that most of the exceptions conform, more or less closely, to the confrontation principle. That is, if a statement is made with the anticipation that it will be used as evidence in litigation, it is less likely to be brought within an exception. I have therefore described the confrontation principle as *The Mold That Shapes Hearsay Law*. (Florida L. Rev. 2014) Many years of development of hearsay law amid inattention to the confrontation principle have weakened this relation, but it is still apparent.

A. Spontaneous declarations and statements of present personal condition (FRE 803(1), (2), (3))

In the early years of the 19th century, as the rule against hearsay took form, courts recognized that some utterances might be so much a part of the incident at issue that evidence of them would be proper. For example, a witness might testify that she heard a cry of "Fire!" as she passed a building and that this caused her to go into the building to lend assistance. The term *res gestae* was often used to cover such purportedly non-hearsay uses of the evidence. Over the course of the century, courts gradually loosened up, so that by 1900 it became clear that they were allowing evidence of some statements made during or shortly after an event for their narrative value – that is, they were being excepted from the hearsay rule. Commentators debated what the better basis for admitting such statements was. In one view, it was their contemporaneity, which meant that the hearsay danger of failed memory never became a concern. An alternate view emphasized the impact of stress and excitement on the declarant, which was thought to minimize the chance that the statement was a fabrication. Ultimately, the FRE adopted both theories, creating hearsay exceptions for *present sense impressions* in Rule 803(1) and for *excited utterances* in Rule 803(2).

The stated rationales for the rules are open to doubt. Absence of memory concern is significant, but that in itself hardly makes a statement particularly reliable. Moderate stress may increase acuity, but great stress tends to diminish it, and in most circumstances even a person under stress can recognize her self-interest and be motivated to act on it very promptly. What we can say is that these rules originated in conformity to the confrontation principle, but that eventually they drifted away from it. And that loosening continued apace after creation of the FRE. Rule 803(1) excepts a statement describing an event or condition made "while or immediately after the declarant perceived it," but courts have sometimes fitted within it statements made minutes or hours, and occasionally (with child declarants) days afterwards. Rule 803(2) applies to a statement "relating to a startling event or condition, made while the declarant was under the stress of excitement that it caused." Note how much more lax this Rule is than its original rationale would suggest: It only requires that the declarant be "under the stress of excitement" caused by the startling event or condition, not that the effect be so great as to preclude reflection and corroboration. Domestic violence prosecutors especially found these exceptions very useful; indeed, they often preferred what came to be known, by a rather bizarre twist, as "evidence-based prosecutions," defined by the one piece of evidence that was *not* presented: live testimony of the complaining witness. The *Davis-Hammon* tandem decision (see pp. 16–17) has restricted use of the technique but hardly eliminated it.

The hearsay exception for statements of mental, emotional, or physical condition (FRE 803(3)) is in a sense a subset of the exception for present sense impressions. That is, the exception covers statements about one's "then-existing" condition, so these are present sense impressions in which the impression is about one's own self. So the rule allows statements of the sort "I feel ... ," "I remember ...," and "I believe ..." to prove what the declarant felt, remembered, or believed, at the time, respectively. Though occasionally courts have pushed the exception to statements of past condition ("I believed ..."), the FRE version of the exception clearly does not extend that far.

Note also that the rule does *not* allow statements of memory or belief to prove the factual proposition remembered or believed (except for one narrow qualification related to the declarant's will). That limitation makes sense, because absent it a statement of the form "I remember X" would be able to do in two steps what the hearsay rule prevents an assertion of X from doing in one: Under the exception, the statement of memory would prove that the declarant remembered X, and from there the inference could be drawn that if she remembered X then X would more likely be true.

And the hearsay exception itself makes good sense for at least three reasons. First, ordinarily these statements, looking inward and contemporaneously rather than reporting on the outside world, are not testimonial. Second, often the best evidence of a person's state of mind or body is what the person says about it; of course, she could be lying or speaking unclearly, but ordinarily at least the danger of misperception as well as of failed memory is eliminated (though, perhaps under the influence of Broadway song writers, I have often wondered whether that holds when one says, "I am [or am not] in love"). And finally, as noted above in Chapter 5, given that introduction of a statement of a proposition X to prove not X but the declarant's state of mind with respect to X is not hearsay, it would be absurd if a tack-on such as "I believe ..." would render the statement inadmissible hearsay to prove the declarant's belief in X.

Now let's talk about one particularly interesting and important application of this exception, associated with the famous case of *Mutual Life Insurance Co. v. Hillmon* (1892). Sallie Hillmon sought to recover on insurance policies on the life of her husband John. But the insurers contended that, rather than having died, John had killed one Walters for insurance fraud, and that a body found near Crooked Creek in Colorado was that of Walters rather than of Hillmon. The case had a long and convoluted litigation history, with six trials and two trips to the Supreme Court, during the first of which, after deciding a procedural issue, the Court announced the evidentiary rule that has made the case famous. On retrial, the Court said, the insurers should be allowed to present evidence that some days before the body was found Walters had written his sister and his fiancée from Kansas, expressing an intention to travel west to Colorado and other places with "a man by the name of Hillmon" who intended to start a sheep ranch. (145 U.S. at 288) Intention, the Court indicated, is a state of mind, and so "evidence that, shortly before the time that other evidence showed that he went away, he had the intention of going, and of going with Hillmon, ... made it more probable both that he did go and that he went with Hillmon than if there had been no proof of such intention." (*Id.* at 295–96)

Let's first think about the core idea – that Walters's statement of intention to go to Colorado is admitted to prove the truth of the statement, that he intended to go to Colorado, and that therefore he did more probably go there. The first step is, as the Court suggested, an ordinary one concerning a statement of state of mind. Assuming that Walters did indeed make the statements (which has been contested), there is no real problem of perception or of memory; he presumably knew what he intended as of the time he spoke. But the inference from his intention to his actual conduct is a most uncertain one; he could have changed his mind subsequently, or something could have intervened to prevent him from acting as planned, and certainly in evaluating these possibilities it would be helpful, were it possible, to have Walters testify live. And yet these are not hearsay problems as such, because they have nothing to do with whether his assertion was true; they are ordinary problems of inferential uncertainty that juries routinely have to handle as best they can. So the hearsay rule does not exclude a statement of intention offered to prove that the declarant in fact had the intention and acted in accordance with it.

Now let's look at the extended reach of the doctrine – the Court said that Walters's statement was admissible not only to prove that Walters went to Colorado but also that he went *with Hillmon*. Given that another person's prospective conduct is involved, this is a statement of more than the declarant's intention, and the legislative history of FRE 803(3) reveals considerable, and unresolved, resistance to this kind of application of the *Hillmon* doctrine. For example, in the most common type of case, a declarant states an intention of meeting with another person and that other person is later accused of kidnapping or murdering the declarant. Suppose (1) there is plausible evidence that the other person intended to meet, or was in a place where the meeting would occur if the declarant came there, and (2) it is not a foregone conclusion that the declarant intended to meet. Then the declarant's statement of intention has substantial probative value even without relying on the declarant's perception of the other person's intention. So, Larry's statement, "I'm going to meet Angelo at his home," increases the probability that the meeting occurred, without relying on Larry's perception of Angelo's intention, given that home is a plausible place for Angelo to be. But if Larry says he intends to meet Angelo in the parking lot of a restaurant that Angelo is not known to frequent, the probative value of the evidence would seem to depend in significant part on Larry's understanding that Angelo intends to meet him. But even in such situations, courts have been willing to admit the evidence. (*See United States v. Pheaster* (9th Cir. 1976).) Niceties of fine doctrinal points aside, it bears emphasis that statements of this sort are almost certainly not testimonial. So in my view courts are stretching doctrinal boundaries to admit evidence that, in a more flexible framework, would be regarded as presumptively admissible because not testimonial.

B.   Statements for medical diagnosis or treatment (FRE 803(4))

This exception grew out of the one for statements of bodily condition, with which it overlaps, in the 20th century. It is narrower than the older one because it only applies to statements made for purposes of "medical diagnosis or treatment." (FRE 803(4)) But it is broader because it is not limited to statements of current personal condition; it also covers statements of past condition and the "general cause" of symptoms or sensations. The exception is based on the perception that a patient has a "strong motivation to be truthful" when speaking to a medical care-giver (Advisory Committee Note to Fed. R. Evid. 803(4)) – a useful ideal, to be sure, but perhaps a curious notion when one recognizes how often patients lie to their doctors.

The exception developed during a period of general inattention to the confrontation principle, and it reaches some statements that a reasonable person in the position of a declarant who has been injured would realize are likely to be used in litigation. Thus, for example, it covers statements made for purposes of diagnosis as well as treatment, and so appears to cover statements made to a doctor who has been hired as an expert for litigation and so will make a diagnosis. Indeed, the Advisory Committee explicitly said that the exception reaches "statements to a physician consulted only for the purpose of enabling him to testify" (*id.*), though occasional courts have said that for the exception to apply the diagnosis that will be made by the care-giver to whom the statement is addressed must be for the ultimate purpose of treatment.

> The statement must be made to a medical care-giver, but that need not be a physician; a child can make a statement to her parent for purposes of medical treatment.

The reach of the exception to statements of the "general cause" of the patient's condition also means that it covers many statements that explain how injuries that are the subject of litigation occurred. The Advisory Committee explained that a patient's statement that he was struck by a car would qualify, but not the assertion that the car had run through a red light; there may be here a glimmer of a sense that admitting such a statement would essentially allow the patient to testify through the care-giver. Statements identifying the person who caused the injury would ordinarily fall outside the "general cause" provision. But in cases of sexual abuse, especially child sexual abuse, some courts have concluded that if the perpetrator is a family member then identification is important to giving proper care, because of the emotional harm that is a virtually certain consequence. Most of these courts, but not all, insist that for the exception to apply to such an identification statement the significance for care-giving must be made clear to the speaker.

C. Business and public records, and their absence (FRE 803(6)–(10))

Businesses keep records and rely on them in their affairs. Sometimes, facts reported in these records become relevant to litigation. For example, in antitrust litigation a party might want to show what its sales were over a given period. Under the exception for routinely kept records (sometimes referred to as business records), it could introduce the records to prove the matter. The rationale usually given is that if the business finds the record sufficiently trustworthy to rely on it, then courts should be willing as well. I believe another significant factor is that, if the record is usually made and kept as a matter of routine, *and if that routine does not include preparation for litigation*, then it is not testimonial. As the exception is stated in FRE 803(6), it does not have a qualifier expressly for litigation-related documents. It does have an open-ended provision allowing the opponent to prove that for some reason the document should not be regarded as trustworthy, but before *Melendez-Diaz v. Massachusetts* (see p. 18), most courts had little hesitation about invoking this exception in support of admitting forensic lab reports and other documents routinely prepared for use in prosecution. That decision has severely restricted the practice but has not eliminated it altogether.

> Notice the differences between this exception and the one for past recollection recorded. That exception does not require that the document have been of a type routinely made, but it requires that a person who made or adopted the memorandum testify at trial, and in the FRE version it only allows the text of the document to be read into evidence.

For this exception to apply, it is not necessary that a person who made, or adopted, the record, testify at trial. And indeed, there may have been many hands in making the document. If the proponent can show that it was a regular practice of the business to make records of that type (and I am using "business" as a shorthand for any ongoing "calling" or organized activity) and that the ultimate source of the information was an acceptable one – more on that soon – then the exception will apply, assuming the opponent doesn't show untrustworthiness. The traditional procedure is to have a custodian of documents, or someone else who is familiar with them, testify live to establish the predicates for the exception. But under an amendment made in 2000, the FRE allow that witness, instead of coming to court, to complete a certificate attesting to the predicates – so one document is being used to get another document into evidence, without any live testimony.

> At the same time, another amendment allowed the underlying document, if supported by such a certificate, to be deemed self-authenticating. I think that if a prosecutor uses this procedure and the certificate is actually presented to the jury (which should not ordinarily be necessary), there is a confrontation problem, because the certificate is plainly created in contemplation of litigation; thus far, the courts seem untroubled.

FRE 803(6) requires that the ultimate source of the information be "someone with knowledge." The identity of that person does not have to be known, and it could be that the information was passed from one person to another, or through a series of records. The Rule does not explicitly require that the person who is the ultimate source of knowledge have been within the organization, but that was the prevailing doctrine before the FRE, under *Johnson v. Lutz* (NY 1930), and it appears that the rulemakers meant to adhere to it. Thus, for example, if a customer provides information to the business and an agent of the business records it, that would not bring the statement within the exception. But some courts have been generous in applying the exception nevertheless if the business took some steps in reliance on the information. Compare CJA 2003, s. 117, which allows the original source of the information to be outside the organization, so long as that person (who need not be identified) "had or may reasonably be supposed to have had personal knowledge" of the information.

Traditionally, and under FRE 803(8), there is also a hearsay exception for public records. This one has a broader scope than the exception for business records in that there is no need for the record to be routinely kept. Consider the facts of *Beech Aircraft Corp. v. Rainey* (1988). A Naval training airplane crashed, killing an instructor and her trainee, and the surviving spouses sued the aircraft manufacturer. The Supreme Court held that under what is now Rule 803(8)(A)(iii) a Navy investigative report could be introduced in support of its conclusion that pilot error, rather than equipment malfunction, was the most likely cause of the accident. That Rule provides a hearsay exception for a record of a public office that sets out, "in a civil case or against the government in a criminal case, factual findings from a legally authorized investigation." The qualifying clause is notable: It seems to reflect recognition that use of such a report against a criminal defendant would violate his confrontation rights. But note also the Rule's reference to "factual findings." Wasn't the conclusion of probable pilot error really an opinion? The Rule did not create such a distinction, said the Court; conclusions drawn by reasonable inference from the evidence may be considered factual findings.

The other principal provision of Rule 803(8), subdivision (A)(ii), excepts a public record that sets out "a matter observed while under a legal duty to report, but not including, in a criminal case, a matter observed by law-enforcement personnel." Here again, we see some recognition of an accused's confrontation rights. So a police report recording observations actually made by an officer would be excepted from the hearsay rule in a civil case, but not in a criminal case.

The FRE also include an exception (Rule 803(9)) for public records of births, deaths, and marriages, "if reported to a public office in accordance with a legal duty." Note that this exception extends to statements made *to* the public office by outsiders. In nearly all cases, the statements are not testimonial in nature and do not threaten the confrontation principle.

Finally, the FRE also include supposed exceptions (Rule 803(7) and (10)) for the *absence* of a routinely-kept or public record. If one would have expected an organization or public office to record a given occurrence if indeed it happened, but there is no such record, then the absence may be proven in support of the proposition that no such incident occurred. The logic is clear enough. The oddity, though, is that if there is no statement then there really is no hearsay problem to begin with.

D.   Statements against interest (FRE 804(b)(3))

If little George admits to chopping down his father's cherry tree – and if we can be confident that no undue pressure was brought on him – the statement seems very likely to be accurate. George may be disinclined to make the statement even if it is true, but he is presumably much less likely to make the statement if it is false; sure, he could be a masochistic, patho-logical liar, or have someone to protect, but it appears that the likelihood ratio of this statement with respect to the proposition it asserts is very high. The traditional hearsay exception for declarations against interest, expressed in FRE 804(b)(3), reflects this perception. That Rule provides an exception for a statement that "a reasonable person in the declarant's position would have made only if the person believed it to be true" because it was so contrary to some interest of the person's; more below on what interests qualify. The logic of the exception is sufficiently persuasive that one might wonder why the exception applies only if the declarant is unavailable as a witness.

Bear in mind that this exception is not necessary if the statement is offered against the declarant himself, because then it would be a party admission.

You will sometimes see the term "admissions by interest," but you should avoid it, because that conflates the doctrine traditionally known as party admissions with this exception for declarations, or statements, against interest.

If one were to list the powerful interests that might dissuade a person from making a self-disserving false statement, the interest against criminal punishment surely would rank high. (Nevertheless, false confessions are a serious problem, far more common than is usually recognized (*see, e.g.,* commentary by Samuel Gross and Maurice Possley, https://tinyurl .com/bd2nck45).) And yet, traditionally, penal interests did not invoke the exception; only pecuniary and proprietary interests did. This occasionally led to great injustices. For example, in *Donnelly v. United States* (1913), the defendant, accused of murder, was not allowed to present evidence that another person, by then deceased, had confessed to the crime. Why were penal interests not covered? I believe it is because often the shoe is on the other foot: One former confederate makes a statement that inculpates both him and the ultimate defendant against whom the statement is offered. As noted above (pp. 54–55), in the *Case of Thomas Tong* (1662), the judges of the King's Bench made clear that a confession could be used against the confessor but not against others whom he implicated. A rather ham-handed way of implementing this straightforward application of the confrontation principle, when the rule against hearsay came to dominate the field, was to make the exception for declarations against interest inapplicable to statements against penal interest, no matter who the offering party was.

That was not a persuasive solution, and it ultimately met resistance. Rule 63(10) of the original Uniform Rules of Evidence (URE) (1953) extended the exception to statements that exposed the declarant to criminal liability, and also to statements that would expose the declarant to "hatred, disgrace or social disapproval." The Advisory Committee to the FRE followed this model, but Congress deleted the latter clause. (California and Kansas retain such clauses.) Also, the Committee, in the Preliminary Draft that it published in 1969, qualified the approach with respect to criminal liability by providing that the exception would not apply to a statement that was offered against an accused and inculpated both the declarant and the accused. That qualification, which basically expressed the principle of the *Tong* case, became a significant source of contention, and it did not survive the final enactment of the Rules.

In fact, the Rule as enacted contained a curious provision that if the statement inculpated the declarant and *exculpated* the accused, it must be supported by corroborating circumstances; such statements, like that of the confessor in *Donnelly*, were thought to be suspect. But isn't the premise of the exception supposed to be that statements against interest are reliable? And was it the statement itself or rather the evidence that it was made that was deemed suspect – and if the latter, why could that not be tested like any other in-court testimony? In 2010, the provision was amended, so that it applies generally to statements tending to inculpate the declarant.

> Third-party statements that exculpate the accused are still generally not within an exception for statements against interest under English law – but they could be admitted under the broad discretionary power given by CJA 2003, s. 114(1)(d), and if the confessor is unavailable (a necessity for the American exception to apply), then under the general exception provided by s. 116, the hearsay rule would not be an obstacle to admission.

Whether the making of a statement should be deemed to have been against the declarant's interests must be determined on the basis of the particulars of the case, and one of those particulars is the audience of the statement. The Advisory Committee to the FRE suggested that a statement implicating both the speaker and another person and made to an acquaintance would ordinarily have no difficulty in qualifying but that the same statement if made while in custody might fail to qualify because it was "motivated by a desire to curry favor with the authorities." That assertion is open to some question from both ends. True, in some circumstances a speaker would hesitate to acknowledge commission of a crime to an acquaintance, but if the speaker is confident that the acquaintance would not pass the information on then the acknowledgment might not be against interest. Indeed, the speaker may have reason for the acquaintance to believe she committed a crime even if she did not do so; in her circles, commission of a crime may be a valued credential. And, while the "curry favor" concern certainly has significance in some settings, in others it seems quite weak. Consider, for example, *Lee v. Illinois* (1986), in which the declarant admitted his complicity in a brutal double murder; it would be hard to avoid characterizing such a statement as being against interest. Of course, the real reason to exclude a statement like that is the one that was recognized in *Tong*: Admitting the statement would allow a witness in effect to testify against a criminal defendant without confronting him, by making her statement privately to the authorities.

The "curry favor" concern is part of a broader issue: Some in a series of assertions may be against interest while others are either neutral or positively in favor of interest. What then? The Supreme Court took a surprisingly rigid view on this question in *Williamson v. United States* (1994). One Harris, arrested after 19 kg of cocaine were found in the trunk of his car, made statements acknowledging his role in a distribution conspiracy and attributing the leading role, as well as ownership, to Williamson. Harris refused to testify at Williamson's trial, and the prosecution offered his post-arrest statements as declarations against interest. The Supreme Court, however, held that a "statement" within the meaning of the exception is "a single declaration or remark," not the extended narrative of which it is a part. (512 U.S. at 599) Thus, if the narrative mixes self-inculpatory statements ("I did it!") and non-self-inculpatory ones ("Williamson did, too!"), it is only the former that are admissible under the exception. Such an approach appears to put great weight on the precise wording of the statements. The Court noted that "Sam and I went to Joe's house" might be deemed against interest if being linked to Sam and Joe would implicate the speaker in their conspiracy. (*Id.* at 603) But then would a court have to break up "Sam went to Joe's house. I went too," and treat only the latter part as against interest? Or would the former part still be considered against interest because it "g[a]ve the police significant details about the crime"? (*Id.*) Arguably, a better analysis would be to ask whether, given that the declarant made the against-interest assertion, it appears unlikely that she would have made the other assertion unless it were true.

In any event, under today's law Harris's statements would pose an altogether different problem: They were clearly testimonial, so after *Crawford* their use against Williamson would be deemed (putting aside any questions of forfeiture) a rather obvious Confrontation Clause violation. Perhaps the Court was motivated by an implicit sense that admitting the statements would effectively allow Harris to testify against Williamson by speaking in private to a drug enforcement agent. If so, *Williamson* was decided a decade too early; had the case arisen after *Crawford*, the confrontation issue would have been glaring, and there would have been no need to undercut the usefulness of this hearsay exception.

E.   "Tender years" exceptions

Beginning in the 1980s, most American jurisdictions created so-called "tender years" hearsay exceptions for certain statements by children. The FRE contain no such exception, and the state provisions, frequently adopted by statute, vary widely. Most of them apply principally to statements by children who have not reached a designated age; 13 years old is a typical maximum, but some statutes set higher or lower limits, and many of them apply as well to statements by other persons who are developmentally disabled. Many of them apply only to statements describing abuse that the child suffered or observed. Often they apply only if the child testifies as a live witness or is deemed unavailable to do so. Usually they either require a judicial determination that the statement is trustworthy or are rendered inapplicable by a determination of untrustworthiness. Some of them apply only in certain types of proceedings, but virtually all apply to criminal proceedings, and some of them are very clear that they apply to statements made to investigators.

So these exceptions, nearly all of which were adopted before *Crawford* and bear the hallmarks of the previous era's reliability-testing approach to confrontation, remove a hearsay bar from statements that, if they were made by adults of ordinary understanding, would plainly be deemed testimonial for purposes of the Confrontation Clause.

What are the consequences if these provisions are applied against a criminal defendant? In *Ohio v. Clark* (2015), the Supreme Court held that statements made by a three-year-old to staffers at his preschool, identifying the person who had hit him, were not testimonial. The majority asserted that the statements "occurred in the context of an ongoing emergency involving suspected child abuse," despite the fact that the child was safe at the time and the alleged abuser was nowhere near. The conclusion that the statement was not testimonial is easy enough to defend – and the Court was unanimous on the point – but the majority's analysis is troubling.

Note the receptive treatment given to such statements in England and Wales, under the Youth Justice and Criminal Evidence Act (YJCEA) 1999 and CJA 2003, s. 120.

Suppose the child were 12, or 17, and made similar statements to a school staffer. It would have been obvious to the child, and to her audience as well, that the statements would likely be used in prosecuting the alleged abuser. Such statements, in my view, should be deemed testimonial, even though they are not made to law enforcement authorities.

A more satisfactory resolution, I believe, is to recognize that a very young child is incapable of being a witness within the meaning of the Confrontation Clause, because she does not understand the gravity of the consequences of her statements. But she is still a source of evidence, and as a matter of due process an accused should have some opportunity to examine her. That opportunity need not be through cross-examination by a lawyer in open court, an exercise that, with respect to very young children, is usually fruitless and often grotesque. A better system would be to allow an examination out of court by a qualified forensic examiner, pursuant to an approved protocol. (Elaboration of this idea may be found in Friedman & Ceci, *The Child Quasi Witness*, U. Chicago L. Rev. (2015).)

Should the accused have a right to select such an examiner? I believe so. But note the Norwegian system for cases of child sexual abuse, in which an expert appointed by the court typically conducts the interview, which must ordinarily be held within two weeks of the report of the crime; after the interviewer takes the child's account, the judge, prosecutor, and defense counsel can ask that further questions be put to the child. (See Phoebe Bowden, Terese Henning & David Plater, *Balancing Fairness to Victims, Society and Defendants in the Cross- Examination of Witnesses: An Impossible Triangulation?* Melbourne U. L. Rev. (2014).) Note also that YJCEA 1999, s. 29 provides for questioning through an intermediary. And under s. 55, the testimony of children under 14 is not sworn.

F.   The residual exception (FRE 807)

Perhaps your head is spinning with this jumble of hearsay exceptions. But wait! There is one more, the most wide-open of all – the residual, or catch-all (or, if you prefer, garbage-bag) exception.

Before codification, courts always had power to adjust the rules of evidence by the ordinary common-law processes. Accordingly, there was no closed list of hearsay exceptions; a court could decide that a given type of statement, or a particular statement, should be excepted from the rule. The initial drafts of the FRE maintained this flexibility: After stating the rule against hearsay, they articulated general principles that should guide a court in deciding whether a statement should be admitted notwithstanding that it was hearsay, and they offered non-exhaustive lists of examples of the types of statements that might qualify. The applicable standards varied depending on whether the declarant was available to be a witness at trial. Thus, Rule 8-04 in the Reporter's First Draft removed the hearsay bar if the declarant was unavailable and the circumstances under which the statement was made offered "assurances of reasonable accuracy." (Would that have been better if it were "reasonable assurances of accuracy"?) By contrast, Rule 8-03, applicable without proof that the declarant was unavailable, made a hypothetical comparison, providing that the hearsay rule would not exclude a statement if there were "assurances of accuracy not likely to be enhanced by calling the declarant as a witness."

This fundamental structure remained through the Preliminary Draft, which was published for comment in 1969. But then, in a Revised Draft (1971), the Advisory Committee altered it by turning the *examples* of evidence that, although hearsay, should not be excluded by the rule into two sets of defined *exceptions* to that rule. For one set, in Rule 803, the availability of the declarant was immaterial, and for the other, in Rule 804, unavailability was required. At the same, the Revised Draft added to each of those two rules a generalized residual exception, Rules 803(24) and 804(b)(5). Even those remained controversial through the enactment process; the House attempted to delete them, but the Senate restored a version of them, and the conference committee added a requirement of pretrial notice.

> Notice requirements are a common feature of modern evidentiary rules.

The two residual exceptions were articulated in identical terms – the differentiation in mode of analysis that was central to the earlier drafts was lost. Each excepted from the hearsay rule a statement that was not covered specifically "by any of the foregoing exceptions" but that was supported by "comparable [changed before enactment to 'equivalent'] circumstantial guarantees of trustworthiness." But what did that mean? There were 23 "foregoing" exceptions listed in Rule 803, four more in Rule 804, more yet if you counted subparts, and they were supported by a wide range of (supposed) rationales. Was a court supposed to compare the given statement to some median standard of exceptions, a different one depending on whether or not the declarant was available? And then in 1997, the two residual exceptions were combined into a new rule, FRE 807, purportedly to facilitate the addition of new exceptions to Rules 803 and 804 (a scary thought!) – which meant that now a court supposedly had to compare the given statement to a standard cobbled together from (at least) 27 exceptions.

In determining trustworthiness, most courts, but not all, considered corroborating evidence if it existed. Why wouldn't they, given that corroboration can be a powerful support for the truthfulness of a statement? Interestingly, there was support for the restrictive view under the old Confrontation Clause regime of *Ohio v. Roberts*, which preceded *Crawford*. If a statement did not fit within a "firmly rooted" hearsay exception, the court had to determine whether it was supported by "particularized guarantees of trustworthiness." The Supreme Court held that this branch of the doctrine, which resembled the residual exception, could not be satisfied by corroborating evidence, but only by "circumstances that surround the making of the statement and render the declarant particularly worthy of belief." (*Idaho v. Wright* (1990)) One might surmise that this limitation made the doctrine seem less like an *ad hoc* determination of whether the specific statement was in fact accurate and more like the development of a category that could ultimately become a new hearsay exception.

Another recurring issue concerned statements that were in the general realm of one of the enumerated exceptions but not quite within it. Some courts thought that such "near miss" statements could not be within the residual exception, because Rule 807 applied only to statements "not specifically covered" by Rules 803 and 804.

When the residual exception was first adopted, the Advisory Committee expressed the anticipation that it would only be used rarely. *That* plainly didn't happen; before *Crawford*, for example, some courts found the exception hospitable to grand jury testimony (not subject to cross-examination) by unavailable witnesses. But courts still professed reluctance to invoke the exception.

An amendment adopted in 2019 made the residual exception more generous, and less structured, in several respects. For good cause shown, notice may be given during trial rather than before. Perhaps most importantly, the exception now explicitly allows for corroborating evidence to support a finding of trustworthiness. Instead of speaking of statements "not specifically covered" by the enumerated exceptions, Rule 807 now speaks of statements "not admissible" under those exceptions, making clear that characterizing a statement as a "near miss" does not in itself preclude the court from applying the residual exception to it.

> Note that the Rule really should not speak of whether statements are "admissible" under an enumerated exception; a hearsay exception means that the hearsay rule does not exclude the statement, but it does not remove other bars to admissibility.

And finally, the amended Rule broke out of the conundrum of assessing "equivalent" guarantees of trustworthiness by speaking instead of "sufficient" guarantees. So now a federal court is not supposed to use other exceptions as a yardstick. But at least arguably this leaves us with another problem: The Rule doesn't state *any* standard as a yardstick. Put another way, sufficient for what? Ultimately, the answer is probably *sufficient for admission*, which is another way of saying that the Rule tells trial judges, "Admit the evidence, notwithstanding that it's hearsay, if you think that it's good enough to warrant admission."

So does that turn the whole complex structure of the rule against hearsay into a sham? I think it's too early to tell. It is doubtful that in the near term the courts will use the residual exception willy-nilly, admitting hearsay evidence whenever they think it is more probative than prejudicial (which, I believe, would be most of the time that live testimony of the declarant would be more probative than prejudicial). But it could well be that over time courts come to rely more and more on the residual exception, making the whole system of exemptions, and indeed the rule itself, far less important.

And then comes a heretical question: Would that be a bad thing? As long as the confrontation right is separately protected – and in proposing the 2019 amendment the Advisory Committee took care to note that "the independent requirements of the Confrontation Clause must be satisfied" – I think it might actually be the best way to go. More on that later.

11 A possible transformation of hearsay doctrine

Few knowledgeable observers are happy with the American law of hearsay as it stands. The law is remarkably complex. It excludes evidence that should be admitted. And it does little to protect any legitimate concern. Small wonder that much of the common-law world has severely restricted the rule against hearsay, especially in civil cases.

And yet I believe that at the heart of the hearsay rule is a very important concern, what I have called the confrontation principle: A witness, especially a prosecution witness, should testify in the presence of the adverse party, under oath and subject to cross-examination, and if possible at trial. For many years, that principle was obscured by the hearsay rule, which has a much broader reach – to all out-of-court statements – but only creates a rather weak presumption against admissibility. But now, in the United States, *Crawford* has protected the confrontation right for criminal defendants independently of the hearsay rule. If there is no need to rely on the hearsay rule to do the work that the confrontation right should do, then it may be that the hearsay rule will become far less structured and much less important. It is significant that the European Convention on Human Rights (ECHR) now provides some protection of confrontation rights even though most judicial systems under the Convention have nothing resembling the hearsay rule; common-law systems would do well to move in that direction.

Continental systems do have a principle of immediacy, but in my view that is not a hearsay rule as such but a partial step in the direction of the confrontation principle. It provides that courts must examine the sources of evidence, including documents, rather than secondary accounts.

That does not mean that hearsay other than testimonial statements offered against an accused would always be admissible. What would an ideal hearsay regime look like? Let's look first at *non-testimonial* hearsay. When a declarant is unavailable, the question seems to be simply whether the evidence is more probative than prejudicial, because the choice is between the hearsay and nothing at all from the declarant. Jurors appear not to have difficulty discounting hearsay to take into account the fact that the declarant is not present and subject to cross-examination. Accordingly, if live testimony of the declarant would be more probative than prejudicial, then presumably the hearsay evidence is as well.

I have elaborated further on this approach in *Jack Weinstein and the Missing Pieces of the Hearsay Puzzle*, DePaul L. Rev. (2015).

If the declarant is available to be a witness but the proponent chooses not to present her, I believe the evidence still should be presumptively admissible, but the situation is more complex. The proponent has chosen not to present the best possible evidence: even if the statement is better evidence than live testimony of the declarant, the live testimony supplemented by the statement is presumably better still. That may be a cost-effective decision; whatever incremental value the live testimony has may not be worth the expense of bringing the declarant in. And if the opponent thinks it would be worthwhile, then in most cases the opponent could produce the declarant as a witness. But opponents hardly ever do so; it is much riskier putting on the stand as your own witness someone who has made an unhelpful statement than it would be asking some questions on cross, and taking whatever gains you may be able to make. Accordingly, I believe that a simple procedural rule would be very helpful: If the opponent, having been given notice of the proponent's intention to use a hearsay statement, produces the declarant, willing and able to testify, then the proponent must produce the declarant as a witness or forgo use of the statement. Given this procedure, the court should usually be willing to admit the hearsay. But it should take into account such factors as how likely presence of the declarant would enhance the jury's ability to assess whether the statement is true; how difficult it would be to produce the declarant; and whether the opponent has been given adequate notice. The admissibility of most evidence is determined under a wide-open, discretionary approach exemplified by FRE 403. It should not be startling to subject non-testimonial hearsay to a similar approach.

Thus, under this system, there would be no need to distinguish sharply between statements asserting a proposition and conduct that appears to reflect the actor's implicit belief in the proposition.

And what about testimonial hearsay? If it is offered against a criminal defendant, then the confrontation right comes into play, and barring for-feiture (or qualification as a dying declaration) it ought to be inadmissible. But what if it is offered by the accused, or in a civil case? Let's first assume that before the opponent had an opportunity for cross-examination the witness became unavailable, through no fault of either party. So the choice is between admitting the testimonial statement – perhaps an affidavit – for what it is worth, and not hearing from the witness at all. I think it would be reasonable to give the court discretion to decide whether an impaired loaf is better than no loaf at all.

> Under South African law, the admission of hearsay is discretionary, in both civil and criminal cases. In my view, that is an excellent solution with one enormous caveat: It provides essentially no guaranteed pro-tection of a criminal defendant's confrontation right. Much the same could be said of the broad discretion provided by CJA 2003, s. 114(1)(d).

And if the witness is available? Let's suppose that the opponent (1) has notice of the proponent's intent to offer the statement and (2) is as able as the proponent to produce the witness, and suppose also that the court adopts the procedural tweak suggested above, under which if the oppo-nent produces the witness able and willing to testify then the proponent must put her on the stand or forgo use of the hearsay. Given that civil liti-gants have ample opportunity to learn information in discovery, and that a prosecutor, representing the power of the state, is in an especially strong position to learn material information, I think it might be appropriate in some cases to say to the opponent, "The proponent is willing to rely on this affidavit rather than bringing the witness in, and that decision seems reasonable. If you think it's worth the trouble and expense of bringing her in, go ahead, and if the proponent doesn't put her on the stand then I'll exclude the evidence, but otherwise I'll admit it."

This, of course, is only one vision of how American hearsay law might change over time. But it is likely that within a generation or two that law will look very different from the way it does today.

12   Character, similar occurrences, and habit (FRE 404-406, 413-415)

When we want to know how a person is likely to act, or have acted, on a given occasion, we will often want to know how that person has acted on similar occasions. So when a prosecutor wants to prove that an accused committed the crime charged, she will naturally want to prove that he committed similar crimes in the past, or otherwise acted in a way manifesting bad character. But in general, such *propensity evidence* is excluded: You cannot prove that a person acted in a given way on a particular occasion by presenting evidence that he acted that way on other occasions or by demonstrating that such conduct is in accordance with his character. (FRE 404(a)(1), (b)(1)) That is the rule, but there are exceptions and ways around it. This chapter will explore all three – the basic exclusionary rule, exceptions to it, and other ways in which it is avoided.

A.   Character in issue

First, let's take into account a basic limitation on the scope of the rule against propensity evidence: It does not pose a limitation when the character of a person, or the person's reputation, is *itself* an element of a claim or defense. In a libel case, the character of the plaintiff, and his reputation, may both be elements of a defense; if the plaintiff deserved the insults the plaintiff threw at him, there is no valid claim, and even if there is one he may have minimal damages if he has a rotten reputation. This means the defendant has to be allowed to prove the plaintiff's terrible character, just like any other fact. And, though a prosecutor ordinarily should not be allowed, in attempting to prove that Dennis committed battery on the occasion charged, to introduce evidence that Dennis has done so on prior occasions, if Dennis is litigating a child custody case the court should give considerable weight to those past batteries. Rather than just trying to reconstruct a past event, the court has to make a forward-looking judgment, whether Dennis is a fit parent. His character, and past acts that might cast a light on it, may be crucial in that task.

B.   The basic exclusionary rule (FRE 404(a)(1), (b) (1))

The discussion here focuses on the core application of the propensity rule, to evidence of bad acts offered against an accused. But the rule is a general one, applying in civil as well as criminal cases, to evidence offered by any party, and to evidence of good as well as of bad character.

Now let's focus on a situation in which the propensity rule *does* apply. At the outset, though, note that Rule 404 does not use the term *propensity*; instead it speaks of *character,* and subsection (b)(1) provides that other acts are "not admissible to prove a person's character in order to show that on a particular occasion the person acted in accordance with the character." But suppose the prosecution, offering Dennis's past batteries to show that he committed battery on the occasion charged, argues, "I'm not trying to prove anything about the accused's character. I just want to prove that he has committed batteries in the past and so is more likely to have committed the battery charged here." This behaviorist argument would not succeed; the exclusionary rule bars the evidence even if no mention of character is made. But however the rule may be characterized, why *should* the evidence be excluded?

One concern is that the jury will overvalue the evidence. I tend to discount this concern. Now of course the fact (if it is indeed a fact) that the accused has committed similar acts in the past does not *prove* that he committed the act charged, in the sense of making it virtually certain, but it does make that proposition more probable.

To say that is not to ignore the importance of complicating factors. Situations matter: A person who will commit a misdeed in one situation may not do so in another. People change over time. And there may appear to be a good deal of randomness in people's behavior – which may mean that the explanations are too deep and too complex for us to understand

– so that a person's conduct on one occasion is an unsure guide to his conduct on another.

But all that having been said, people's characters have a good deal of coherence and stability. Most people would not consider committing armed robbery, under virtually any circumstance. The fact that the accused did commit armed robbery in the past may make it far more likely that he would do it on the occasion in question. Even if a crime has a low recidivism rate, Roger Park has pointed out, what really matters is what might be called the *comparative commission rate*: Even if, say, only 5% of those who commit a crime will commit it again, if only .001% of the general population ever commits the crime, then evidence of a prior commission may be highly probative.

So if evidence of a prior bad act were admitted against an accused and the jury gave it considerable weight, how can we say that the jury would give it *too much* weight? What is more, exclusion could not be justified by the mere conclusion that the jury would overvalue the evidence, because exclusion guarantees that the jury will in effect drastically *under*value the evidence, giving it no weight at all; exclusion would be warranted on this basis only if we believed that in some sense the jury was likely to give the evidence more than double its "true" weight, whatever that may be, and I don't believe we have any grounds for concluding that this is so.

But there is another ground that I do believe provides strong support for the propensity rule. Learning that the accused committed bad acts in the past is likely to *bias* triers of fact (whether judge or jury) against him, making them more likely in effect to punish him for his past misbehavior and also to convict if satisfied to a standard of persuasion lower than the prescribed "beyond a reasonable doubt." And add to this the time and distraction that proof of the prior acts could entail; instead of being a trial about whether the accused committed the crime charged, it might, absent the rule, turn into a crime about whether he is a bad person.

C.   Exceptions (FRE 404(a)(2), 413–415)

Among the exceptions to the propensity rule is a complex set of provisions that allows some evidence bearing on a witness's character for truthfulness or untruthfulness to be admitted for purposes of assessing the witness's credibility. These rules are best treated as a separate topic, and we will examine them in Chapter 15.

1.   Prior sexual misconduct

Some jurisdictions maintain an exception, in cases in which the charge is sexual misconduct, for at least some prior sexual misconduct by the accused. The longest-standing version of this exception is one maintained by some jurisdictions for evidence demonstrating a "lewd [or lustful] disposition" (*e.g.*, *Soper v. State* (Alaska Ct. Apps. 1992); *Ballard v. Hunt* (W.V. 2015)) or a "depraved sexual instinct" (*e.g.*, *Dillard v. State* (Ark. 1998)). When the exception is termed this way, it is principally applied to cases of child sex abuse. The impetus behind such rules appears to be that, although this is propensity evidence, it is particularly strong, because most people do not have such a sexual disposition and, absent the evidence, the jury might have trouble believing that the accused would find sexual appeal in children. That idea raises some troubling issues: Does it depend on a perception that, say, rape of a young adult woman would seem more comprehensible to a jury than would child sexual abuse, because it is more like robbery, the taking of something that it is not unusual to want but by improper means? In 1994, the U.S. Congress weighed in, and through the legislative process added three rules to the FRE, Rules 413–415, which provide a broad exception to the propensity rule for prior acts of sexual misconduct and child molestation. Some states have followed along. The political support for making prosecution of these crimes easier is clear; less clear is whether there is any good justification for excepting these particular crimes from the general propensity rule.

2.   Character of a criminal defendant

Under a longstanding rule, now expressed in FRE 404(a)(2)(A), an accused, unlike any other party, may put his character into play on a propensity theory; he may offer general evidence of a pertinent trait of his character to show that he is unlikely to have committed the crime charged. The rule allows an accused to say, in effect, "I'm not the type of person who would have committed this crime." Courts are sometimes generous in determining what a pertinent trait is. Most defendants do not take advantage of this rule, because if a witness testifies to the good character of the defendant the prosecution will be allowed to cross-examine on the basis of the defendant's bad acts and to put on witnesses as to his bad character; it is a general principle that, even if only one party may initiate proof on an issue, once proof is presented an adversary must be allowed to present rebuttal evidence.

Under English law, even if the accused does not present a character witness, if he has no prior convictions (and perhaps even if he has a record that is deemed of peripheral importance) he may be entitled to an instruction advising the jury that it may take his good character into account.

3.   Character of a victim

A traditional rule also allowed a criminal defendant to present evidence of a pertinent trait of a victim's character. As a practical matter, this rule applied in two basic settings. One occurs when the accused, charged with rape, contends that the alleged victim's prior sexual history suggested an exculpatory explanation, such as that she had actually consented to sexual conduct with the accused. "Rape shield" laws, such as FRE 412, severely limit the use of evidence in this context; I will postpone discussion of these to Section G below.

The second setting occurs when the accused, charged with a violent personal crime, contends that the victim was the first aggressor. In this setting the accused can introduce evidence that the victim was a person of violent character. And if he does so, the prosecution may naturally introduce rebuttal evidence, to prove that in fact the victim was a person of gentle disposition. (FRE 404(a)(2)(B)(i)) As the result of a 2000 amendment, the FRE now also give the prosecution a "You're one to talk!" option in that situation: The prosecution can introduce proof that the *accused* has a violent character. (FRE 404(a)(2)(B)(ii)) In some settings, this rule might not be justifiable. Suppose the prosecution contends that the accused killed because of a longstanding grudge, but the accused contends that he acted in self-defense after the victim became enraged over something the accused said; then it would not appear that impugning the character of the victim should open the door to evidence of the accused's character. But it's probably fair to say that in most cases, if the victim's hotheadedness is sufficiently probative on the self-defense issue to warrant admissibility, then the relative hot-headedness of victim and accused is fair game.

> FRE 404(a)(2) refers throughout to an "alleged victim." I'm not bother-ing with the adjective in that context; if somebody gets killed or badly hurt, I figure he's a victim even if he deserved it. Use of "alleged" would seem more appropriate in FRE 412, because often a rape defendant contends that no crime was committed – but that Rule just speaks of a "victim."

Another traditional rule, now stated in FRE 404(a)(2)(C), provides that *in a homicide case* if the accused contends that the victim was the first aggressor, then the prosecutor may present evidence of the victim's peaceful character. Note that this rule does not require that the accused have raised the character issue; it is enough if he simply contends that the victim cast the first blow.

So each of the rules discussed in the last four paragraphs gives the accused the option of pulling a trigger, by raising an issue, and if he does so the prosecution may respond; the trigger and the permissible response vary from one rule to another.

D.   Methods of proof (FRE 405)

We have seen that, despite the propensity rule, the character of a person may be proved in several settings; character itself may be an issue in the case, or one of the exceptions may apply. So then the question arises of *how* character may be proved. FRE 405 addresses that.

First let's assume that a trait of a person's character may be proven and rebutted because one of the exceptions applies; let's say the accused is trying to prove how gentle he is and the prosecution wants to rebut that. (The same general principles apply with respect to the other exceptions, but it will be easier focusing just on one.) The accused can't present a witness, even himself, to testify to gentle things he has done (assuming they're not otherwise relevant to the case), and similarly the prosecution can't present a witness to testify to violent acts of his. The fear is that if such particularized proof of matters collateral to the case were allowed it could take over the whole trial. So each side is limited to proving general assessments. The traditional rule was even more restrictive: A witness could not testify, "In my opinion the accused is a gentle person," but instead had to testify to something like, "In our community the accused has a reputation for being a gentle person." The thought was that different people might have different opinions of a person's character, but the person would have only one reputation throughout the community. Well, the rule is odd right off the bat, because reputation is hearsay, and often based on multiple layers of hearsay. But beyond that, if a witness thought well of the person in question, then almost inevitably she would testify that he had a sterling reputation; the restriction did little but create awkwardness in testifying. So FRE 405 changes the common-law rule; it doesn't bar reputation testimony, but it allows opinion testimony as well, and witnesses usually testify that way, which is most natural for them. Most states have followed along.

But let's say a neighbor of the accused has told the prosecutor about all sorts of violent things the accused has done. The prosecutor can't put the neighbor on the stand to testify to those, but if the accused does dare to put on a character witness, then the prosecutor can cross-examine her on the basis of those acts. To be technically precise, the questions should be of the form "Do you know ...?" if the witness has testified to her opinion of the accused, and "Have you heard ...?" if she has testified to his reputation. And here is an oddity: If the witness answers in the negative, the prosecutor has to "take her answer"; she *still* can't put the neighbor on the stand to testify to the violent deeds. That gives an opportunity for a witness who knows the rules of evidence and is willing and able to lie with a stone face. More significantly, it puts an ethical burden on the prosecutor. She can't just make up stuff. ("Do you know about his 17 axe murders?" ... "No?" ... "Just curious.") So she had better have some supporting evidence in her pocket, literally or at least figuratively, in case the court calls her to account.

Now let's suppose that character is itself an issue in the case. Then it may be proven like any other issue, which means that the proponent may build proof brick by brick. That means that the proponent can introduce evidence of particular acts that demonstrate the character trait in question. And, just for good measure perhaps, FRE 405 also allows the proponent in that case to introduce summary evidence of opinion or reputation.

E.   Other purposes for offering other-act evidence (FRE 404(b)(2))

Remember that the propensity rule is not a general prohibition against proof of uncharged bad acts; it only bars the use of those acts when offered on a propensity theory, to show that the accused (or any other person) acted in accordance with the propensity suggested by the other acts. Prosecutors therefore often are highly motivated to find some non-propensity theory on which the evidence might be admissible. FRE 404(b)(2) provides a non-exhaustive and overlapping list of some of these purposes: "proving motive, opportunity, intent, preparation, plan, knowledge, identity, absence of mistake, or lack of accident." Sometimes these are spoken of as if they are exceptions to a rule of exclusion. But this is a misconception. Rather, these are *ways around* (end runs once again!) a relatively narrow exclusionary rule; there is no closed list of such uses.

Since 1991, if the prosecution wants to invoke FRE 404(b)(2), it must give notice to the accused. The notice provision does not apply in civil cases.

So, for example, suppose the charge is murder. The prosecution will have a legitimate desire to prove that the accused had a motive for the murder. If that motive was to cover up an earlier crime to which the murder victim was a witness, then the prosecution ought to be able to prove that crime. Or if the accusation is bank robbery, the prosecution ought to be allowed to prove that the accused stole a car, either beforehand or afterwards, to help him make a getaway. Or if a celebrity is accused of improper touching during a photo session with a fan, a history of such touching may help dispel a contention that the contact was accidental.

That last illustration is an example of what is sometimes called the "doctrine of chances." More dramatic are cases like the notorious one of the "Brides in the Bath" (*R. v. Smith* (Crim. App. 1915)). Smith, charged with murdering his new wife for financial gain, contended that she had suffered an epileptic seizure in the bathtub. Evidence that two subsequent wives had died in similar circumstances helped send Smith to the gallows. Repeated instances of similar events suggest that the most parsimonious explanation is not a series of random occurrences but a similar design, repeatedly implemented. So this appears on close inspection to involve a propensity inference as part of the reasoning. But the most salient aspect of the logic is the comparison to the hypothesis that the charged incident was an accident, and courts have usually had little hesitation in admitting evidence on this basis; it is not quite the same as asking the jury to rely on other incidents to conclude, say, that the charged incident was rape rather than consensual sex.

The structure of the rules often sets up an odd dynamic in which the prosecution claims that it needs to present evidence of a prior bad act so that it can prove some fact that the defense contends the prosecution has no need to prove. Suppose the defendant is charged with having committed burglary by cutting a chain-link fence with metal shears, and the prosecution wants to prove that he committed other robberies in a similar manner. Now, everyone in the courtroom will understand that the prosecution's real hope is that if the evidence is admitted the jury will quite naturally give it substantial weight on a propensity theory. But the prosecution cannot argue for admissibility on that basis (and in fact it is hoping that the jury will ignore an instruction not to draw a propensity-based inference from the evidence). So instead, the prosecution might contend that it needs the evidence to prove that the defendant had the knowledge and ability to cut a chain-link fence with metal shears. Defense counsel might respond that this is nonsense because just about anybody can cut a chain-link fence. *Perhaps* the court will say that the prosecution's rather minimal need for the evidence is outweighed by the potential that the jury will use it on an improper, and therefore prejudicial, propensity basis. But if the case involves safe-cracking, instead of fence-cutting, the court would be more likely to rule in favor of the prosecution. Note that in either case, defense counsel, recognizing that the evidence is dangerous and the issue of ability is a loser anyway, might even stipulate that the accused had the ability in question. Such a stipulation does not necessarily resolve the matter; courts often say that prosecutors must be allowed to prove their cases in the way they choose.

Sometimes prior bad acts are offered to prove identity. The logic usually is that it appears probable both that the same person committed both the crime charged and the uncharged act and that the accused committed the uncharged act, so the evidence makes it more likely that the accused committed the crime charged. And probably most often the basis for the first part of this syllogism is that there are rare similarities between the two acts, so rare that the manner in which they were committed constitutes a *signature* or *earmark*, or a unique *modus operandi*, of the perpetrator. The parties often contest whether the similarities are so strong and rare as to justify this inference. That two robberies both occurred in late afternoon in suburban banks by men wearing masks and gloves should not qualify; however, that during two bank robberies the robber forced tellers to undress so that he could photograph them would qualify.

Unfortunately, courts often slide over into treating *modus operandi* as being a valid point of proof for the prosecution in itself, even when identity is not at issue. That is usually little more than dressing up propensity evidence with another name. The same thing frequently happens when prosecutors offer evidence to prove a *common plan or scheme*. If, say, an accused is charged with fraudulent security sales to a given customer, it would be valid to prove that the accused sold similar securities to customers as part of a single overarching scheme: It may be that attempting such sales would not be profitable unless the perpetrator were able to take advantage of economies of scale, effectively amortizing the startup costs of the plan over many customers. If that is *not* the theory – if it is just that the accused succeeded in one commission of a crime and so repeated the pattern – that seems to be nothing more than propensity evidence. But courts often accept this argument, most notably in cases of sexual misconduct (in states that do not have an exception to the propensity rule for such conduct).

F.   Habit and routine practice (FRE 406)

There is in effect another limitation on the propensity rule. If in a given situation a person acts habitually in a particular way, then evidence of that habit may be introduced to prove that the person acted in that way on the occasion in question. It is hard to deny that a habit is a propensity, albeit a very strong one. So what distinguishes a habit, which may be admitted under FRE 406, from an excluded propensity? The line is fuzzy at best. The Reporter's first draft offered a definition, as "a course of behavior of a person ... regularly repeated in like circumstances"; although the Advisory Committee deleted this definitional section, it points to two factors that taken together will tend to qualify a pattern of behavior as a habit: the *specificity of the stimulus* and the *regularity of the response*. Suppose, for example, the question is whether Defendant came to a full stop when he drove up to a blinking red light on State Street at the corner of Washington Street. Evidence that Defendant is a careful (or careless) driver would be subject to exclusion under the propensity rule; evidence that Defendant almost always came to a stop at blinking red lights would probably qualify as a habit; and evidence that he always stopped at the blinking red light at State and Washington certainly would. And FRE 406 treats "an organization's routine practice" on a par with "a person's habit." So if a party wants to prove that on a given occasion the organization acted in a particular way – say, by immediately sorting all incoming mail – but no witness is able to testify to that fact, the inference can be drawn from proof that this is what it does as a routine matter.

It is sometimes said that habit refers only to relatively simple, non-volitional activity, but that seems to take too narrow a view of the matter. Perhaps there is merit in the more moderate view that conduct is more likely to be considered a habit the more reflexive and automatic it is, and the less thought and planning it requires. But I wonder if that is simply because more complex decisions are less likely to exhibit sufficient regularity of response. In any event, bright lines are hard to draw. I go out for a long walk almost every morning, often on the same route to Gallup Park, and I don't usually do a lot of thinking about it before I head out. But sometimes I vary the route, and occasionally – as on the very day I'm writing this – I decide not to go. (I'm playing pickleball this afternoon; I'll get enough exercise.) So do I have a habit of walking in the morning, and of walking to Gallup Park?

The answer should probably depend in part on the purpose for which the evidence is offered. If I suddenly disappear, and the person accused of kidnapping me was seen waiting in a car in Gallup Park around the time I often get there, then evidence that I frequently walk to the park at that hour would be highly probative – even if my routine is far from uniform. On the other hand, if I am accused of having attended a conspiratorial meeting at a neighbor's home, my contention that this could not be because I go walking at that time of day would not have much weight at all unless I could prove that my practice was invariable. And even then it might not be worth much, because (even if my routine could be described as non-volitional) I could always decide that the lure of the conspiracy is strong enough to warrant a one-time departure.

As Rule 406 was presented to Congress, it contained a subsection on methods of proof, providing that habit or routine practice could "be proved by testimony in the form of opinion or by specific instances of conduct sufficient in number to warrant a finding that the habit existed or that the practice was routine." The House Judiciary deleted the provision, saying that the method of proof should be left to the courts on a case-by-case basis. But the Uniform Rules of Evidence (URE) retained the provision, and, though most states have not adopted it, it reflects the generally tolerant manner in which courts tend to look at habit and routine practice. Evidence of one or two instances will not be deemed sufficient. Particularized evidence of numerous instances should usually be acceptable, but most often the proof of habit comes in the form of an overall assertion of the habit by a witness who was in position to observe it on numerous instances, without detailing specific instances; that witness could be the person whose own conduct is at stake.

G.   The rape-shield laws (FRE 412)

The original Advisory Committee that drafted the FRE took it as a matter of course that a person accused of rape and contending that the sexual conduct was consensual could, pursuant to the same principle that governs the self-defense cases, present evidence of a pertinent trait of the alleged victim. In this setting, that evidence was usually proof that she had a prior sexual history, and most often it was offered to prove that she more likely consented to sexual contact on the occasion in question. But in the 1970s, even as the FRE were being considered, social attitudes in this area changed dramatically and with them so too did the law. Ultimately, every state adopted some form of "rape shield" law, with many variations among them. A federal version, Rule 412, became one of the earliest amendments to the FRE, added in 1978. For simplicity, I'll focus on that one.

Applicable in any case involving alleged sexual misconduct but subject to some exceptions, FRE 412 generally excludes evidence of a victim's other sexual behavior or her sexual predisposition.

Rule 412 applies whichever party wishes to offer the evidence; English law is more tolerant of the prosecution in a rape case offering evidence that the complainant's background suggests she would not have been predisposed to have consensual sex with the accused.

Rules of this sort perform several important purposes. First, in most cases, the alleged victim's prior sexual behavior or disposition has little probative value with respect to the issue of whether she consented to sex on the occasion in question. Second, the evidence may be prejudicial. I have discounted the importance of jury overvaluation as a basis for evidentiary rules. Perhaps it has some explanatory force in this context, but more important, I think, is the possibility that the evidence will cause some jurors to devalue the complainant. Third, the rules play a valuable expressive role, emphasizing that whatever the complainant did on prior occasions does not diminish her right to be protected against rape. Fourth, an inquiry into the complainant's prior sexual history and predispositions may be traumatic and will likely feel like a grotesque intrusion into her private life. And finally, the prospect of such an inquiry may create an additional disincentive – on top of fears of mistreatment by the authorities and of retaliation by the police – to reporting the crime. (The impact of the rape-shield laws in increasing reporting appears to have been modest, but it should not be ignored.)

So there does not seem to be any real debate nowadays about the appropriateness of rape-shield laws. And yet a complete prohibition on this type of evidence would be going too far. FRE 412(b)(1)(A) and (B) list two narrow exceptions for criminal cases, both limited to specific instances of the alleged victim's sexual behavior. First, theoretically it could be that evidence of other sexual conduct will help the accused make it appear plausible that someone else was the source of semen or injury; the injury cases did not arise often, and in an age of ready DNA testing a semen case would be quite extraordinary. (The prosecutor may also offer such evidence, if it happens to help her case.) Second, and more importantly, prior sexual conduct *with the accused* may be offered by the accused to show consent. Obviously, consent on one occasion does not mean that the complainant consented on the occasion in question. But if the two had a prior consensual sexual relationship, that might make the accused's contention that the conduct charged was in fact consensual appear more probable – enough so that it would be unfair to allow the accused to be convicted without him being able to inform the jury of that history. Suppose the alleged victim testifies that the accused walked into her office and kissed her without any invitation to do so; a juror's assessment of that evidence may be affected by learning that the two had been sleeping together. In particular, if the accused and the two were married, though that does not at all preclude the possibility of rape, it is a fact that the jury ought to know.

Subsections (A) and (B) of FRE 412(b)(1) do not exhaust the possible circumstances in which fairness requires that the accused be allowed to present some evidence of the complainant's prior sexual history, and so subsection (C) provides an exception to the exclusionary rule if "exclusion would violate the defendant's constitutional rights."

Subsection (C) might appear superfluous; if exclusion would violate the accused's constitutional rights, then FRE 412 could not mandate exclusion. But Rule 412(c) requires a party who wishes to invoke one of the exceptions in Rule 412(b) to file a motion specifying the evidence and also to notify the victim or the victim's guardian or representative. By explicitly providing for cases in which the accused has a substantive constitutional right to present the evidence, the Rule makes clear that these procedural requirements apply to those cases.

Note also that *R. v. A. (No.2)* (H.L. 2001) achieved much the same result as subsection (C) by invoking Article 6 of ECHR. This doctrine might be applied in cases involving prior sexual history between the complainant and the accused, for which English law has no specific provision.

These cases can be excruciatingly difficult; courts need to be very hesitant to admit this type of evidence, but the accused may contend that assessing the exculpatory story that he tells requires understanding some aspect of the complainant's sexual activity. Consider two examples. Occasionally, an accused contends that the complainant accused him of rape because she had become pregnant by her boyfriend, and given the religious beliefs of her family she could not admit to them that she had had consensual sex. And in *Olden v. Kentucky* (1988), the accused contended that he had consensual sex with the complainant but that she accused him of rape because she had an extra-marital affair with the accused's half-brother and the half-brother had seen them together in circumstances that would make him suspect that she was unfaithful to him; the Supreme Court held that the accused had a constitutional right to present this evidence. Unfortunately, there is no substitute in this realm for careful and sensitive analysis of the facts of each case.

The presumptive prohibitions of FRE 412 apply in civil cases as well as criminal ones, but more softly, given the wide range of circumstances that might arise. Subdivision (b)(2) creates a kind of reverse version of Rule 403, allowing evidence of an alleged victim's sexual behavior or predisposition if its probative value substantially outweighs potential negative consequences. But only an alleged victim may present evidence of her reputation; this serves as a reminder that the Rule is meant to make the litigation experience easier for alleged victims.

13 Other categorical exclusionary rules (FRE 407–411)

This chapter addresses several other categorical exclusionary rules. These rules have a common structure. They each bar some form of evidence from being introduced for a given purpose, but not for other purposes. They are sometimes justified in part on the basis that the probative value for the prohibited purpose is not great and the potential for prejudice is greater, but for most of them the more persuasive reason is that they prevent the prospect of admissibility from inhibiting socially beneficial behavior.

A. Subsequent remedial measures (FRE 407)

Suppose a customer slips and falls on a store's tile floor. After the accident, the store replaces the floor with a less slippery one. The customer sues the store for his injuries. At trial, his lawyer offers evidence of the replacement, arguing, "See? They knew the floor was dangerous. That's why they changed it. If they had made the change earlier, my client wouldn't have been injured." But under a longstanding rule, expressed in FRE 407, evidence of such a subsequent remedial measure would not be admissible.

Why not? One argument is that the evidence might have limited probative value, and perhaps significant prejudicial potential. In a negligence case, a subsequent remedial measure has little bearing on whether the defendant was on notice before the accident of the dangerous condition; it may be that it was the accident itself that gave the store notice that the tile floor was dangerous. As the 19th-century English judge George Bramwell said, it is a mistake to conclude that "because the world gets wiser as it gets older, therefore it was foolish before" (*Hart v. Lancashire & Yorkshire Ry. Co.*, 21 L.T.R. N.S. 261, 263 (1869), quoted in Adv. Com. Note to FRE 407).

But notice is not the only issue in a negligence case, and if the defendant is strictly liable for injury resulting from a dangerous condition, notice does not enter in at all. Does the fact that the defendant corrected the condition after the accident indicate that the condition was dangerous? There are various reasons why a store might replace a floor – it could have been merely a cosmetic matter, and the timing may have been purely coincidental – and so safety considerations may have had nothing to do with the change. And yet, depending on the circumstances, the evidence might tend rather strongly to prove that at least after the accident the defendant recognized that the pre-accident condition was unsafe; indeed, the jury may regard such an *admission by conduct* as having particular significance. Just because the defense is able to state alternative explanations does not mean that they are persuasive – the usual response when a party raises alternative explanations for apparently damaging evidence is to say, "Tell that to the jury," not to exclude the evidence.

Another explanation often given for the rule is that admissibility of the evidence would disincentivize the socially beneficial conduct of taking remedial measures that might prevent similar accidents in the future. In some settings, that argument might be persuasive; if the lawsuit is for a large amount, and the accident is an unusual one that is unlikely to recur even absent remediation, a defendant might hesitate to undertake a measure that would be used against it in the litigation. But most accidents are not of this nature; if it happened once, it could happen again and again. True, a defendant may be concerned that the remedy will be used as evidence against it in a case involving an accident that has already occurred. But even a callous defendant may well decide that it has no real option but to minimize the chance of repetition.

A third possible explanation is that, apart from incentives, it might seem unfair to punish the socially beneficial conduct of remediation. But good deeds do get punished frequently; admitting wrongdoing is a good deed, in part because one understands that negative consequences are likely to follow, but of course admissions are readily admitted. Indeed, a *prior remedial measure*, say adoption of a system that should minimize the chance of an accident, is socially beneficial, but if for some reason the system did not operate on the occasion in question, then the system and its failure would certainly be admissible evidence against the defendant.

On balance, the arguments in favor of the exclusionary rule are probably strongest in negligence cases, where notice is a salient issue; the
subsequent remedy has little bearing on notice but it may distract the
jury. Many jurisdictions have followed the lead of California, and held
the rule inapplicable to manufacturing-defect cases, or more generally
to strict-liability cases. But FRE 407 has moved in the opposite direction. As originally enacted, it was ambiguous on the matter, but a 1997
amendment made clear that the Rule does apply to strict-liability cases.
One may wonder whether, especially as applied in this context, the Rule
gives manufacturers a windfall, excluding potentially persuasive evidence
of conduct that the manufacturer almost certainly would have taken
irrespective of evidentiary consequences. At the same time, the Rule was
amended to clear up an ambiguity: If a product is redesigned, but then
a copy made under the old design is involved in an accident, does the
exclusionary rule apply? Now it clearly does not; under the amendment,
it applies only "[w]hen measures are taken that would have made an
earlier injury or harm less likely to occur." If one really believes in the
incentives-based argument for the rule, this change may have been the
wrong call – a manufacturer will have a disincentive to remedy a problem
if it knows that doing so may be used against it in litigation arising from
accidents involving copies of the old design that are still in use – but it
does mitigate the windfall effect.

In any event, the rule applies broadly to any kind of remedial measure,
such as altering a potentially dangerous condition, redesigning a product,
or revamping a medical protocol. Sometimes defendant organizations
contend that a critical self-analysis – in which members of the organization acknowledged difficulties in its operation and attempted to advance
the process of improvement – falls within the exclusionary rule. Such
contentions pose a quandary. On the one hand, such an analysis is often
an important part of remediation, and so it arguably falls squarely within
the theory of the exclusionary rule, even if it is not the culmination of the
process like a change in product or in operational practice. On the other
hand, an analysis that says, in effect, "We have messed up badly, and we
have to do better!" may be highly probative; it is not a tacit or implied
admission or an admission by conduct, but simply a raw admission, and
potentially a very probative one at that. Courts have most often been
skeptical of applying the exclusionary rule to such analyses; self-criticism
by government agencies seems to have a better chance of being deemed to

fall within the rule, as do evaluative statements as opposed to statements of fact.

The exclusionary rule only applies to the extent the evidence is offered to prove that the defendant acted (or failed to act) in a liability-creating way. It does not apply to other purposes for which the evidence might be offered. FRE 407 provides a non-exhaustive list of illustrations of such other purposes. One is impeachment. If, for example, a defendant in a slip-and-fall case testifies that a photo represents the scene before the accident, the plaintiff could prove that the defendant had removed the tripping hazards before the photo was taken; the fact that hazards not in the picture were previously on the scene would be material irrespective of how they came to be moved, but the fact that *the defendant* removed them has extra impeachment value given his testimony. FRE 407 also lists, as possible uses, ownership, control, and the feasibility of precautionary measures, but only if they are disputed. Thus, if a defendant construction company contends that it had no authority over a section of a highway where an accident occurred, the plaintiff could prove that after the accident the defendant repaired the allegedly dangerous condition. But in our store slip-and-fall case, the plaintiff could not prove as part of his case-in-chief that the floor was in fact the defendant's because after the accident the defendant altered it; unless the defendant challenges the fact, there presumably is no serious doubt that the floor belonged to it, and given the exclusionary rule the plaintiff should not be allowed to evade it by manufacturing an issue he supposedly needs to prove.

As for feasibility, suppose the plaintiff suggests a particular remedial measure that if taken beforehand would have markedly decreased the chances that the accident would occur. If the defendant contends, "Well, we couldn't have done *that*," then the plaintiff ought to be able to respond by proving that it did just that shortly after the accident. But if the defendant contends, "Sure, we had the *technological* capacity to do that, but it wouldn't have made any economic [or medical, or whatever] sense given what we then knew," the question is different. It could be that the accident in question altered the calculus, making what had previously appeared economically prohibitive now appear virtually essential. Consider also a leading case, *Tuer v. McDonald* (Maryland 1997). In accordance with hospital protocol, a doctor preparing heart surgery on a patient ordered that he be taken off a blood thinner several hours before the operation's scheduled time; there were good reasons supporting this decision but also substantial risks, given that the patient had unstable angina. The patient died shortly after the surgery, and soon after that the hospital changed its protocol so that in a similar situation the blood thinner would not be discontinued until the operation was about to start. At trial, the doctor was asked whether it would have been unsafe to maintain the blood thinner longer, and he answered in the affirmative. The Maryland Court of Appeals held that this did not contravene feasibility; the court deemed the defense view to be that such maintenance would have been feasible but, on the information then available to them, not advisable. In its extensive discussion, the court pointed out that especially in strict-liability cases it is often difficult to draw a line between disputing feasibility and simple defense on the merits. The court drew a distinction between "assert[ing] that a given course would be unsafe, in the sense that it would likely cause paramount harm to the patient," and merely asserting that "there was a relative safety risk that [defendants] believed was not worth taking"; the former but not the latter would be deemed to controvert feasibility. As the court noted, in demonstrating a defect, the plaintiff "necessarily injects the question of feasibility into the case," and "the defendant ordinarily responds by showing why those alternatives were not used." Courts have not provided a clear resolution for this perplexity.

B.   Settlement offers and related evidence (FRE 408–410)

1.   Civil settlements, offers, and associated statements (FRE 408)

Let's say Plaintiff, who has brought a civil negligence action for $5 million, rejects a $300,000 settlement offer made by Defendant. The case goes to trial, and Plaintiff offers evidence of the offer. "See," Plaintiff might argue, "Defendant knew he was liable and was willing to pay good money to make this case go away." And correspondingly, if Plaintiff offered to settle the case for $20,000, Defendant might want the jury to know that: "See, Plaintiff knew there was nothing to this case," Defendant might argue. "He was just trying to squeeze whatever he could out of my client."

Traditionally, and under FRE 408, the evidence is not admissible to prove or disprove the validity or amount of the claim. One reason sometimes given is that the evidence has limited probative value. The offer may have been motivated principally by a desire to avoid the distraction, time, and cost, financial and emotional, of litigation; this may be a difficult matter for the jury to assess, and it may consume a good deal of trial time to explore. This rationale may have weight when (focusing for now on Defendant's side) the offer is small, essentially an attempt to get rid of the case for nuisance value. But if, say, the offer were for $3 million, it would be hard to deny its significance in suggesting Defendant's belief in his liability. (Fox News's settlement with Dominion Voting Systems for $787,500,000 sure seemed significant.) The "more consistently impressive ground" for exclusion, as noted by the Advisory Committee, is that exclusion fosters the public policy in favor of settling disputes. If it were not for the rule, a party would have to hesitate, knowing that the very act of making a settlement offer would hand over to the other side a potentially powerful piece of evidence. And so, in keeping with the instrumental impulse behind the rule, it applies however large or small the offer may be in relation to the relief demanded.

Moreover, when a party settles one case, he may be aware that other related ones are in the pipeline. So even if Plaintiff accepts Defendant's offer, Defendant may have to worry that other claimants will seek to use evidence of the offer against him. And so the rule applies to completed settlements as well as to rejected offers, and to other cases as well as the one in which the settlement was made.

For the rule to apply, there must be a genuine dispute over the validity or the amount of a claim. There are two aspects to this. First, the dispute must have gelled into a claim; if, for example, the parties have ongoing business relations and they are trying to work out the state of the account between them, then there may not yet be a claim to be compromised within the meaning of the rule. Second, the exclusionary rule would not apply if the potential defendant offers no reason to doubt either the validity or the amount of the claim and is only trying to minimize the amount he pays the plaintiff.

Settlement negotiations frequently involve not just offers and counter-offers but statements about the underlying dispute, and some of those statements may acknowledge facts that may help the party's adversary at trial. The hearsay rule does not prevent such a statement from being offered against the party who made it, because it is a party admission. And traditionally, the exclusionary rule governing settlement negotiations did not apply to it unless the party making the statement put up some flag such as "without prejudice," "speaking hypothetically," or "for settlement purposes only." The drafters of FRE 408 followed the California Evidence Code in undoing this limitation on the exclusionary rule. The change was a controversial one during the drafting process. The Senate Judiciary Committee, which restored the change after the House had limited it, expressed the view that the traditional rule "constituted a preference for the sophisticated, and a trap for the unwary." (Sen. Rep. 93-1277 (1974)) Another view of the matter is possible: To the extent the exclusionary rule is meant to incentivize participation in compromise negotiations, it can have that effect only on a party who is aware of the rule in the first place. Therefore, especially given the great probative value that these admissions often have and to avoid giving a windfall to a party who was oblivious to the rule, it might be appropriate to require a party relying on the rule to demonstrate that by a clear signal before making the admission.

It is important to recognize that the rule excludes evidence only when offered to prove or disprove the validity or amount of the claim or, under a 2006 amendment to FRE 408, to impeach by a prior inconsistent statement or a contradiction. If there are other material propositions to which it might be relevant, the rule simply does not apply. FRE 408(b), which provides a non-exhaustive list of some purposes for which the evidence may be offered, unfortunately terms them "exceptions," but they are not; they are simply purposes that might warrant admitting the evidence and that lie outside the scope of the exclusionary rule. The purposes listed by that subsection are "proving a witness's bias or prejudice, negating a contention of undue delay, or proving an effort to obstruct a criminal investigation or prosecution." These might occur, respectively, if a defendant reached an unduly generous settlement with a claimant who later became a witness for him; if protracted settlement negotiations dispel a claim of failure to prosecute; and if the defendant attempted to buy off a potential criminal complainant.

So the exclusionary rule doesn't apply to impeachment by bias but it does to impeachment by prior inconsistent statements and contradiction. Why? The Advisory Committee explained that it feared that the latter forms of impeachment would swallow the rule; imagine a party testifying arguably in variance with a statement he made during negotiations.

2.   Criminal pleas, negotiations, and associated statements
      (FRE 410)

FRE 410 is in a way a criminal counterpart to FRE 408, in the sense that it excludes some evidence related to attempts to resolve a criminal case. To start, it provides that in any proceeding, evidence of a guilty plea that was later withdrawn or of a *nolo contendere* (no contest) plea, whether or not withdrawn, may not be admitted against the defendant who made it. (Note that in one sense this exclusion is broader than that of Rule 408, and most of the other rules being considered in this chapter; it is not confined by the purpose for which the evidence is offered.) A guilty plea on which a judgment of conviction was entered does not fall within this Rule; after all, that is about as much of an admission as can be imagined. So why is a *nolo* plea, which also allows a conviction to be entered, excluded? In jurisdictions that allow such a plea, the essential purpose is to allow the defendant to resolve the criminal case, by not resisting the conviction, without prejudicing his interests in any other litigation that might follow. After an accident that injured many people, for example, the defendant might find it worthwhile to resist the civil suits against him but not the criminal charges. Rule 410 also presumptively excludes a statement made during a proceeding on each of the excluded types of pleas; the policy behind this provision is clear enough, because the exclusion of the pleas would be of little benefit if statements made during the required associated proceedings were admissible. And further, the Rule presumptively excludes statements made to *an attorney* for the prosecution during plea discussions if they did not lead to a guilty plea on which a judgment of conviction was entered. The limitation to statements made to an attorney is meant to ensure that, for example, statements made by the accused to the arresting officer, in an attempt to bargain down the charges, do not qualify; it is only plea negotiations within the relatively formal channels ensured by attorney participation that do.

Rule 410(b) provides two exceptions. First is a rule of completeness: If, say, the defendant is able to introduce a statement made during a plea discussion, then that opens the door to another statement made during that discussion "if in fairness the statements ought to be considered together." And second, if the defendant is subsequently charged criminally with having made a false statement during plea negotiations or proceedings, and the statement was under oath, on the record, and with counsel present, he cannot invoke Rule 410 to keep the allegedly false statement out of evidence.

Sometimes a prosecutor tells the accused that, as a precondition to entering into settlement discussions, the accused must agree to waive his rights under Rule 410. Suppose, then, that the case does not settle and at trial the prosecution wants to introduce a statement the accused made during the failed negotiations. To what extent, if any, should the waiver be given force? In *United States v. Mezzanatto* (1995), the U.S. Supreme Court held that if the accused testifies contrary to the earlier statement, then a waiver could validly allow that statement to be used for impeachment. The logic of the Court's opinion seems to support broader admissibility, as part of the prosecution's case-in-chief, but it did not go that far, because three justices, crucial to forming a majority, reserved the issue. Most subsequent lower-court decisions have upheld full waivers; others, without resolving that question, uphold a waiver allowing the prosecution to use the prior statement to rebut any evidence offered by the accused, including but not limited to his own testimony.

3.   Offers to pay medical expenses (FRE 409) and
        statements of sympathy

FRE 409 also expresses a rule somewhat related to that of FRE 408. It reads in its entirety: "Evidence of furnishing, promising to pay, or offering to pay medical, hospital, or similar expenses resulting from an injury is not admissible to prove liability for the injury." Note that the rules are distinct: Rule 409 comes into play even if there is no claim at the time the conduct occurs, and the conduct does not have to be in consideration for settling a claim. The rule is justified in part on the basis that the evidence might have limited probative value, given that the action may have been motivated by a humanitarian impulse with no hint of an acknowledgment of fault. Perhaps an incentive-based argument provides a stronger basis for the rule, though one may wonder how often parties who make such generous offers are bearing evidentiary consequences in mind. Another argument would be based on moral considerations: Perhaps this is a good deed that *should* go unpunished. That argument, too, can be contested: As noted above, p. 94, admitting fault is also a good thing to do, and of course party admissions are regarded as a particularly valuable form of evidence; sometimes part of doing a good deed is bearing unpleasant consequences. And in fact Rule 409, unlike Rule 408, does not exclude associated statements, which are not essential to the offer. Thus, suppose the full statement is, "I'm sorry we hurt you. We'll pay your medical expenses." The second sentence would be excluded by Rule 409, but the first sentence would not.

Since adoption of the FRE, some states have gone a step further, excluding in a civil action (to quote one common formula) "[t]he portion of statements, writings, or benevolent gestures expressing sympathy or a general sense of benevolence relating to the pain, suffering, or death of a person involved in an accident and made to that person or to the family of that person." (Cal. Evid. Code § 1160(a)) Some of these statutes apply only in the health-care context. Most often, though not always, they also fall short of excluding evidence of statements apologizing or acknowledging fault. Thus, "I'm sorry you're suffering" would fall within such an exclusion. "I'm sorry I hurt you" would not – but it would fall within the exclusion provided by the typical Canadian statute.

C.   Liability insurance (FRE 411)

When a civil defendant is covered by liability insurance, the insurer will presumably pay for at least part of any damages award. A plaintiff might contend that the coverage reduced the defendant's incentive to act carefully, but his real interest in mentioning insurance would be that the jurors are likely to be freer with the insurer's money than with the defendant's. The defendant, making the same calculation, would respond that any mention of insurance is prejudicial. The traditional rule, expressed by FRE 411, resolves the matter by barring evidence that the defendant had liability insurance to prove that he acted negligently or otherwise wrongfully. And for that matter, if the defendant is *not* insured, though he might want to let the jurors know that – on the professed theory that he had a strong motive to be careful, but primarily for the purpose of informing them that he will be bearing the cost of any award – the rule does not allow him to do so. Perhaps the best justification for this exclusionary rule is that, as a matter of law, the jury is supposed to decide the case as if the defendant personally will bear the cost of liability, and mention of insurance can only make this more difficult – though in an age of compulsory automobile insurance and widespread professional liability insurance, savvy jurors will assume in many contexts, without being told, that the defendant is insured.

Like most of the other rules in this chapter, this one excludes the evidence only to the extent it is offered for a given purpose. But if, for example, the defendant calls as a witness an adjuster for his insurance company (which is probably controlling the defense) to give an assessment of damages, the rule will not prevent the plaintiff from pointing out the connection, which demonstrates bias and so may impeach the testimony.

14   Privilege (FRE 501, 502, 612)

The word *privilege* is used in various ways. Here, we will use it in a relatively narrow sense, to refer to rules that exclude evidence of confidential communications within certain relationships. Some of these rules are based on an instrumental rationale, to avoid prospective litigation use disincentivizing the communication. And others are based on a perception that, notwithstanding the basic principle that the law is entitled to every person's evidence, the litigation system should not intrude too deeply into some intimate relationships. Section A of this chapter discusses the most fundamental question with respect to privileges: Should the particular relationship be treated as a privileged one? Sections B, C, and D explore questions related to the bounds of privileges – the usual limitation of the privilege to the content of communications, and the requirements that the communications be made within the course of the designated relationship and that they be confidential. Section E discusses exceptions to privileges, Section F examines the question of how they may be waived, and Section G presents procedural issues governing their exercise.

Privilege is often an intensely controversial and politically inflected aspect of evidentiary law. The drafters of the FRE proposed a comprehensive treatment of the subject, but Congress deleted it, instead providing, in FRE 501, that state law governs privilege in cases where that law provides the substantive rule of decision, and that in other cases, unless otherwise provided by the Constitution, statute, or rule, the common law as interpreted "in the light of reason and experience" determines claims of privilege. The URE adopted a codification of privilege closely modeled on the deleted Federal Rules, and we shall occasionally refer to them here.

A.   Is the relationship privileged?

Suppose you tell your best friend one of your deepest secrets. "You can't tell anybody else!" you say. "Understood," the friend replies. But then she is subpoenaed because your secret turns out to be material to a lawsuit. "That communication was in confidence!" you and she tell the court. "Tough luck," says the court. The law is entitled to every person's evidence, and there is no best-friend privilege.

But over the centuries, courts, legislatures, and rulemakers have decided to treat certain relationships as privileged, which ordinarily means that, no matter how probative certain communications between the persons involved may be, one or both of them have a comprehensive right to prevent disclosure of them, in discovery, at trial, or at any other time. A person who has that right is the *privilege holder*; in privileges based on a professional relationship, the holder is usually the non-professional, but the professional may have an obligation to claim the privilege on behalf of the holder if the holder is not in a position to do so and has not waived it.

The range of privileges and the variations among jurisdictions in implementing them are both so large that it is difficult to make statements about them that hold universally. Accordingly, the discussion here will only give a hint of the complexities in this area.

Perhaps the most important and best established privilege is the one for the attorney-client relationship, and that is the one on which we shall focus most closely. This privilege is based on an instrumental rationale. That is, if it were not for the privilege, many communications between client and attorney would be inhibited, because the client would know that anything she said to the attorney would ultimately be disclosed to her litigation adversary. This instrumental rationale appears to justify the privilege only when litigation is actually proceeding or in the offing; for example, it does not appear that, if a client has a conversation with a transactional lawyer about a deal that does not raise a prospect of litigation in the near future, the absence of the privilege would have much of an inhibiting effect, because the client has information she wants the lawyer to know and the chance of an adverse litigation effect appears small. So arguably the privilege should be limited to communications made in the context of actual or anticipated litigation; communications with other advisors out of the litigation context, such as financial consultants, are not privileged. But there is essentially no chance that this will happen: A privilege comes with some cachet, and lawyers tend to write the rules.

The *work-product* doctrine *is* limited to work done in preparation for litigation. It also does not provide as strong protection as the privilege; it can be overcome in some settings by a showing of need. But it is not limited to, and indeed is not needed for, confidential attorney-client communications. It extends to preparatory work done by any member of the litigation team, including not only the attorney but the client and any representative of the client.

Now contrast the attorney-client privilege with the one for spousal communications. In most contexts, that privilege is not necessary to avoid inhibiting the communication; usually, neither spouse is worried that their conversations are likely to haunt them in later litigation. Rather, the rationale appears to be that it would be unacceptable for the state to intrude into the privacy of communications between one spouse and another.

There is also a related doctrine that limits the ability of a prosecutor to call the accused's spouse as a witness against the accused. In some jurisdictions, the accused can keep the spouse off the stand, and in others the choice is the testifying spouse's. This privilege is not limited to confidential communications; it applies to any testimony the spouse might otherwise give.

Most other privileges are justified by one or the other of these rationales. For example, some jurisdictions recognize a privilege for conversations between journalists and confidential sources, and under American law there is a privilege for confidential communications among the President and his closest advisors. And governments have a privilege to prevent disclosure of the identity of an informant who supplies information about legal violations to law enforcement personnel. (In England and Wales, this area is addressed under the rubric of *public-interest immunity*, previously known as Crown privilege.) These privileges are best supported on an instrumental rationale, the idea being that if the privilege did not exist the communications would be inhibited and perhaps prevented altogether.

Nevertheless, these privileges, unlike most others, can be overcome given a sufficient showing of need.

On the other hand, consider the privileges recognized for communications between a patient and a psychotherapist, or between a communicant seeking spiritual advice and a cleric. (The latter has sometimes been referred to as the priest-penitent privilege; it has perhaps most commonly been invoked with respect to statements made to a priest during the rite of confession, but it applies more generally.) In most circumstances, such communications would not be inhibited if they were not privileged. And if a relatively few would be inhibited because they were made when litigation was proceeding or anticipated, that might not be a terrible loss. (Note the contrary situation with respect to the attorney-client privilege, in which the absence of the privilege would likely impair the prospects of having a fair and accurate determination of the litigation.) Rather, a better justification for these privileges is that, absent them, the state would be intruding unduly on important and intimate relationships – and in the case of the religious privilege concern that the cleric would be forced to violate the precepts of his religion.

In recent years, many jurisdictions have adopted some form of a victim-counselor privilege. Both the instrumental and intimacy rationales might be considered at work here. The covered communications occur after a crime has allegedly been committed, so litigation is clearly anticipated and the privilege may remove an inhibition to frankness. And, though the relationship presumably does not predate the incident, it may concern matters of a highly personal and traumatic nature, and the counselor's success depends on building a trusting relationship.

Now, there are many intimate relationships that are not protected by privileges. For example, in most American jurisdictions, there is no parent-child privilege. And although some states recognize a physician-patient privilege, most common-law jurisdictions do not; even if one is recognized, it does not apply in the most common situation in which a patient might want to invoke it, when the patient's own condition is the subject of litigation, and the significance of this context might explain why most jurisdictions do without the privilege altogether.

B.   The subject matter of the privilege

For the most part, privileges of the type discussed here protect the contents of communications that fall within the privilege. So, for example, the attorney-client privilege protects the *content* of confidential communications between attorney and client. It does not ordinarily protect against disclosure of the *fact* of the communication; in exceptional cases, however, identity is the crucial fact the client is attempting, and is allowed, to shield. And the *information* communicated is not itself privileged.

Suppose, for example, that Adam and Brenda, competing widget manufacturers, meet in an attempt to fix prices, and are later sued civilly. Adam tells his lawyer Linda, "Yeah, we tried to come to an agreement." At deposition, Adam is asked, "Did you meet with Brenda in an attempt to fix prices?" Adam could *not* properly answer, "Sorry, I have spoken to my lawyer on that subject; it's privileged." And if it is established that Adam and Brenda met, privilege probably would not allow Adam to duck the general question, "Did you talk to Linda about that meeting?" But if the question were, "What did you tell Linda about the meeting?", that would be privileged.

Similarly, suppose that during the meeting Adam took down notes about it. He would not make the notes privileged if after being sued he passed them along to Linda; you cannot cover bad information or documents with privilege by passing them along to your lawyer. (And what if he put at the top of the notes: "Privileged and confidential; for legal advice"? That would have no effect unless the court determined that the notes were in fact written for the purpose of transmission to the lawyer.) But if in sending the notes along to Linda he wrote a message to her in the margins, *that message* would be privileged.

Though privileges are generally articulated in terms of communications, in some cases they extend more broadly to information transmittal. This is perhaps most apparent in the case of the physician-patient privilege, where it exists; if the physician learns some information about the patient's condition from examining her, that would be within the privilege, even if the patient did not communicate the information to the physician.

C. The course of the relationship

Privilege only applies if the communication in question occurred in the course of the relationship. For example, a statement to a priest in the confessional would comply; if the same statement were made at a cocktail party, it probably wouldn't, because that is not where priests render spiritual comfort and advice. For the attorney-client privilege to apply, it is not necessary that a formal relationship have already been established at the time of the communication. For example, if a client consults a lawyer in hopes that the lawyer will represent her, that conversation would be privileged even if in the end the lawyer declines the representation. But casual conversation with a friend who happens to be a lawyer would not be privileged unless it is held for the purpose of securing legal services. And sometimes, especially in the corporate context, there are doubtful cases: Was the lawyer acting *as lawyer* in participating in the conversation, or was she really wearing another hat, perhaps as a corporate officer? And was the lawyer really included for the purpose of securing legal advice, or was her name included in an attempt to throw a cloak of privilege over a business communication the participants would like to keep private?

D. Confidentiality

Privilege applies only if the communication was confidential; remember that privilege operates in derogation of the ordinary principle that the law is entitled to every person's evidence, so the law generally takes the view that if you are willing to say something outside of the privileged circle then the judicial process can hear it as well. Suppose you have a conversation, in ordinary tones and seeking legal advice, with your lawyer in the back of an Uber. The driver gives no indication of interest in your conversation, but there is no partition. The conversation would not be considered confidential; the driver *could* listen if she wanted to. And so privilege would not apply. (It would be different if the third person present were an infant or were known not to speak the language.) You, your lawyer, and the driver could each be compelled to testify about what was said.

But that does not mean that for privilege to apply only two individuals can be part of the communication. It may be that others are necessary to facilitate it; that is why I have spoken of the *privileged circle*. For example, if the client and the lawyer speak different languages, then an interpreter may participate in the conversation without impairing the privilege. Or perhaps the lawyer finds it useful to have a paralegal take notes, or either client or lawyer might dictate a note to the other through a secretary. But if Husband dictates to Secretary a message intended for Wife, that will probably not be considered privileged; spouses do not need intermediaries to maintain an intimate conversation with each other.

It is important to recognize that the bounds of privilege and of professional obligations of confidentiality are not co-extensive. The lawyer in that Uber conversation would have an obligation not to divulge to others what she learned from it, even though it was not privileged. And in many professional relationships no privilege exists but an obligation of confidentiality does. There is no privilege for a student's communications with the Dean of Students, for example – but the Dean would have an obligation to maintain the student's confidences. Such obligations would give way, of course, if the law comes calling and demands to know what was said. And, on the other side, whatever the ordinary rules of privilege or of confidentiality might be, in some situations disclosure is authorized or even required under a principle associated with the case of *Tarasoff v. Regents of the University of California* (Cal. 1976) and codified in numerous statutes: If a psychotherapist or other clinician has reason to believe that a patient represents a serious threat to another person, then the clinician may be permitted or required to warn that person or authorities.

E.   Exceptions

Even if a communication is otherwise within a privilege, the privilege may fall within an exception. Exceptions vary widely from one privilege to another, and from one jurisdiction to another. Some exceptions render a given privilege inapplicable altogether in given types of action. For example, some jurisdictions that maintain a physician-patient privilege carve out an exception for criminal cases. And under Uniform Rules of Evidence (URE) 504(d), the privilege for spousal communications is inapplicable, among other settings, in a civil suit between the spouses or

> in any proceeding in which one spouse is charged with a crime or tort against the person or property of the other, a minor child of either, an individual residing in the household of either, or a third person if the crime or tort is com-

mitted in the course of committing the crime or tort against the other spouse, a minor child of either spouse, or an individual residing in the household of either spouse ... .

It is probably evident from the face of this Rule how many choices it reflects; along several dimensions, it is by no means inevitable that rule-makers would choose to go this far and no farther. Compare the more expansive provision in PACE 1984, s. 80(3).

Other exceptions apply to particular types of statements. For example, under URE 502(d)(3), there is no attorney-client privilege "as to a communication relevant as to an issue of breach of duty by a lawyer to the client or by a client to the lawyer." Nor, importantly, does the privilege apply "if the services of the lawyer were sought or obtained to enable anyone to commit or plan to commit what the client knew or reasonably should have known was a crime or fraud."

F.   Waiver (FRE 502, 612)

Now, suppose that a given communication is privileged when made: It was confidential, made during the course of and within the scope of a relationship covered by a privilege, and not within an exception. The privilege may yet be waived.

Waiver can occur in various ways. If the jurisdiction recognizes a physician-patient privilege, it will usually be waived as to consultations the patient had concerning a condition for which he is suing; if the patient is willing to make his condition a matter of litigation, it would be absurd to let him prevent his adversary from learning about consultations he had on that very condition. Similarly, if a client contends in litigation that he took some action on the advice of counsel, then he will be deemed to have waived privilege with respect to those consultations. If a witness refreshes her memory by examining a privileged document while testifying – and sometimes if she does so beforehand – she will be deemed to have waived the privilege. (FRE 612(a)) Probably most waivers are made by disclosure of the privileged conversation.

Sometimes waiver is well considered. A client may direct his lawyer to disclose some matters publicly, or to an adversary. Even if the waiver is not explicitly authorized, it may be that the lawyer can properly waive the privilege as she exercises her best judgment in representing the client; settlement negotiations might involve such implicitly authorized waivers.

But sometimes waiver occurs more haphazardly. Courts have traditionally taken the view that parties must protect privilege as jealously as if it were the crown jewels and run the risk of losing it if an outsider gained access to a privileged communication. For example, in one case, a retailer searched through a distributor's garbage dumpster over an extended period and found numerous documents, some of them subject to attorney-client privilege, that supported its suspicions about the distributor's behavior. The court held that the distributor had lost the privilege; it could have taken more protective measures, such as by shredding the documents. Given the volume and burdens of modern discovery in an era of enormous amounts of electronically stored information, it has become difficult to prevent all inadvertent disclosures of privileged materials – inadvertent, perhaps, in the sense of failure to realize that the document was disclosed or that it was privileged. In recent years, courts and rulemakers have been more generous to parties that have made such disclosures. FRE 502(b), adopted in 2008, provides that inadvertent disclosure doesn't operate as a waiver of privilege if the privilege holder had taken "reasonable steps to prevent disclosure" and afterwards "promptly took reasonable steps to rectify the error." And, under Fed. R. Civ. P. 26(b)(5), if a party that had produced a document notifies an adversary that the document is privileged, the adversary must effectively freeze use of the document until the question of privilege is resolved.

Another frequently recurring issue typically arises when a government agency conducting an investigation seeks privileged documents. The target of the investigation may be willing to disclose the documents to the agency, in hopes of facilitating a resolution of the matter, but unwilling to disclose them to other parties, often because doing so would facilitate lawsuits against it. Should such *selective waiver* be allowed? Traditionally most courts in the United States have said no. (English courts appear to have been more willing to consider the possibility.) Rule 502(d) now provides that privilege "is not waived by disclosure connected with the litigation pending before the court," in which case the disclosure would not be a waiver in other proceedings. This provision appears to have been meant to ease further the problem of inadvertent disclosure, especially in the context of expedited discovery, but it can be read to authorize a court to provide that even intended disclosure of privileged matter to a party before it does not constitute a waiver, so long as the matter is resolved without that party making open use of the matter.

Now let's distinguish selective waiver from *partial waiver*. Suppose a holder discloses the privilege with one in a series of communications. Whether that will be deemed a waiver with respect to others will depend in large part on the context. If the waiver occurred outside the context of litigation, and the holder sought no advantage from it in litigation, then probably the waiver will be limited to the matters that the holder actually chose to disclose. But the holder cannot skim the cream in litigation: If he offers some privileged communications into evidence, then a rule of completeness will apply and the court must decide which other communications in the series ought to be disclosed to prevent unfairness to the holder's adversary.

G.   Procedural considerations

Privilege questions often generate litigation. In some cases, the court might require what American courts call *in camera* review in order to resolve the issue of whether a given communication is privileged; that is, the holder discloses the communication to the court, which reviews it privately, but not to the adversary. Courts are usually hesitant to order such review (and indeed California Evidence Code § 915(a) severely limits the circumstances in which they can), but in some settings it greatly facilitates decision-making.

Sometimes questions arise as to who may – and must – claim the privilege. The holder of the privilege has the choice. Thus, if a person who made a confession to a priest decides to waive the privilege, the priest could not successfully maintain that the sacredness of the confessional precludes him from testifying as to what he was told. But if the holder has not waived privilege with respect to a communication with a professional, and the professional is asked to disclose the communication, she will usually be required to assert the privilege on behalf of the holder. And the attorney-client privilege is usually held to survive the death of the client – but after death, the personal representative of the client's estate steps into her shoes and can decide to waive the privilege.

One could contend that, given that a holder has the option of waiving the privilege, its exercise should support an inference that the privileged communication would have been adverse to the holder's interests. But most American jurisdictions decline to subject the exercise to that cost. They provide that no adverse inference may be drawn from the exercise; therefore, they do not allow the court or counsel to comment on the exercise, and they prescribe that, to the extent practicable, the proceedings should facilitate exercise without the jury knowing about it.

15 Witnesses: competence, impeachment, and support (FRE 801(d)(1)(A), (B), 603, 605, 606, 610, 611, 613, 701)

The common law has always been very dependent on the testimony of witnesses, ordinarily given live in open court, subject to oath and cross-examination. This chapter will first discuss the question of what predicates are necessary for a witness to give her testimony. It will then address the complex topic of how the credibility of a witness might be impeached and supported. Our focus here is on lay witnesses; expert witnesses are discussed in Chapter 16.

A.   Competence (FRE 601-603, 605, 606, 610, 701)

The common law had many rules disqualifying certain categories of witnesses as incompetent. In the early days, parties and their spouses could not testify; indeed, not until 1864 in any common-law jurisdiction was the accused in a criminal case allowed to testify in his own defense (though in earlier times the accused often spoke up without taking an oath).

> Maine was the first to allow sworn testimony by a criminal defendant. England and Wales did not follow suit until 1898. The last holdout, the state of Georgia, was compelled to give up the common-law rule in 1961.

Felons, atheists, agnostics, the mentally disabled, and children deemed too young to take the oath were also all deemed incompetent. Gradually, virtually all these rules of competence washed away, their supposed role in protecting accuracy in fact-finding supplanted by the principle that the trier of fact can take into account any perceived defects in a witness's truth-telling ability. Indeed, FRE 601 provides for federal cases that "[e]very person is competent to be a witness unless these rules provide otherwise" – and the FRE do not include any rules preventing any categories of persons from testifying, except for the presiding judge (FRE 605) and, as a general matter, a juror (FRE 606).

Under FRE 606(b), a juror may testify at trial about any improper outside influence that may have affected the verdict. Also, under *Peña-Rodriguez v. Colorado* (2017), an accused has a constitutional right to present a juror's testimony of racial bias on the jury that may have violated the accused's right to an impartial jury.

With respect to matters of religion, the law has moved even further: FRE 610 now provides that "[e]vidence of a witness's religious beliefs or opinions is not admissible to attack or support the witness's credibility."

There are qualifications, however, to this broad rule of competence. FRE 603 expresses a rule of very long standing, which underlay some of the old incompetency rules, that before testifying a witness must take an oath or make an affirmation that she will testify truthfully. With respect to children, many jurisdictions do not use a formal oath but hold a brief proceeding to try to determine whether the child understands the obligation. Occasionally, the court concludes that the child does not, and so bars the child's testimony; one might ask whether it would be better nevertheless to hear from the child, for what her observations are worth.

Note the discussion on p. 70 of the possibility of treating young children as "quasi witnesses."

Even if there is no rule of incompetence keeping a witness off the stand, there may be a rule rendering her incompetent to testify as to a given subject. For instance:

- A substantial number of jurisdictions bar testimony that has been hypnotically refreshed, either absolutely or absent a demonstration that the hypnosis was conducted in a way to minimize suggestiveness.

- Some courts have kept out testimony of long-ago events that allegedly had been suppressed and then, much later, recovered by a therapeutic intervention, on the ground that the recovery mechanism has not been demonstrated to be sufficiently reliable. Usually the common-law system depends on cross-examination to assess the accuracy of testimony, so such a reliability-based precondition to live testimony is unusual – but then again, so is the phenomenon of memory recovery.
- A few jurisdictions still retain a "dead man's statute." These statutes, which previously were common, vary substantially, but the essence usually is that a party that is litigating against an estate should not be allowed to testify to a transaction with the decedent, given that the decedent's lips are now sealed. Most jurisdictions have done away with these, and for good reason; they exclude highly probative evidence, and it is easy enough, absent such a statute, for factfinders to understand that they are only hearing one side of the story.

The most important and pervasive rule of competence is probably the rule requiring personal knowledge, expressed in FRE 602. Unless the witness is testifying as an expert – a subject discussed in Chapter 16 – she must testify about what she observed with her own senses. Thus, if a lay witness arrives at a scene after an accident, she may testify about what she saw but she may not testify as to her inference about what happened before she arrived. She could, for example, testify to the position in which she found two cars, not to her conclusion that the blue car slammed into the red one. Why not? It is the jury's job to determine what happened, and the witness's job to give the jury the information it needs, which is her actual observances. What those observations were will be obscured if the witness testifies instead to inferences – and if the witness is able to convey to the jury what her observances were, then the jury does not need the inferences.

The difficulty, though, is that to some extent witnesses must draw conclusions. For example, human beings communicate about color, not frequency of electromagnetic radiation. It would be a rare witness who could testify, "The light coming from the car had a frequency of 4.62 x 10^{14} Hz." And it would be nearly as rare that a juror would be able to make any use of that information. But a witness could testify, "The near car was red," and the jury would then have a sense of what the witness was trying to convey. Now, I say "a sense" because problems remain. This witness will necessarily perform two evaluative tasks simultaneously. One is the *choice of a standard* for using particular terms. What portions of the spectrum does the witness characterize as red? The other is *evaluation of the phenomenon.* The witness assembles the information provided by her sensory perceptions and concludes that what she has seen is a car and not, say, a model of one.

And so a practical accommodation must be made. FRE 701 provides that a lay witness may offer an opinion within narrow confines. First, the opinion must be "rationally based on the witness's perception." That is a nod to the personal knowledge requirement, but it suggests some extra leeway; the opinion must be *rationally based on* perceptions, not sheer speculation, but it can be more than a simple *report of* those perceptions. Second, the opinion must be "helpful to determining the witness's testimony or in determining a fact in issue." Whether because of presence at an event or of familiarity with some condition, the witness has information that would be helpful to the jury. The limits of human communicative ability mean that, to give the jury as much as reasonably possible of the information that the witness has, the witness may have to include some evaluations in her testimony. But to the extent she can, the witness should give the jurors the benefit of her observations without adding evaluations.

Under a 2000 amendment, a lay opinion also must not be "based on scientific, technical, or other specialized knowledge within the scope of Rule 702 [on expert opinion]," but that requirement really just assures that the witness is not in fact testifying as an expert.

B.   Impeachment (FRE 607–609)

Because the common-law adjudicative system is so dependent on the testimony of witnesses, it gives leeway to a party who wants to impeach, or undercut the credibility of, a witness, and then to a party who wants to "rehabilitate" the witness, rebutting the impeaching evidence.

A party may not bolster the credibility of a witness before it has been attacked.

Traditional law provided as a general matter that by calling a witness a party "vouched" for her credibility and so, at least unless her testimony surprised him adversely, he could not impeach her. But FRE 607 does away with this rule. A fraud plaintiff, for example, may find it necessary to call the defendant as a witness and then impeach his testimony, and he may do so, even without showing that the testimony was a surprise. There is one limit, however, that courts should carefully monitor. Suppose a prosecutor calls as a witness a former confederate of the accused, knowing both that she has allegedly made a statement implicating the accused and that she will testify contrary to it; if evidence of the prior statement would not otherwise be admissible, and the prosecutor's *purpose* in calling the witness is to introduce that evidence for impeachment, this tactic should not be allowed.

English law retains the traditional voucher rule. But if the accused wishes to call a witness who is likely to be hostile – such as one who made and then retracted a confession to the crime being charged – he can request that the witness be called by the prosecution, which would immediately tender the witness to the defense for cross-examination.

Several methods of impeachment are possible; this brief summary will capture only some of the complexities.

1. Opinion and reputation evidence (FRE 608(a))

Recall from Chapter 12 that in general you cannot demonstrate a person's character to make it appear more likely that she acted in accordance with the character on a given occasion – but that there are exceptions, and one, which we postponed in Chapter 12, is for the character of truthfulness or untruthfulness of a witness. An impeaching party may present a *character witness* to offer an overall assessment – either the witness's own opinion or her report of reputation – of the primary witness's untruthful character. And *if* the primary witness's character for truthfulness has been attacked, the supporting party (usually, but not inevitably, the proponent of the witness) may offer a witness to give a contrary assessment.

2. Misconduct suggesting dishonesty (FRE 608(b))

Evidentiary law aims for a delicate balance, attempting to provide ample room for assessing a witness's credibility but not allowing litigation over collateral matters – in this context, meaning matters that are material to the case only so far as they bear on the witness's character for truthfulness – to dominate the trial. So if you put a character witness on the stand to testify that the primary witness has a dishonest character, you cannot ask her about particular acts of dishonesty that the primary witness has committed. (For the moment, we're putting aside prior convictions of crime; that comes next.) What you can do, in the discretion of the court, is ask the primary witness on cross-examination about those dishonest acts. ("Didn't you lie on your C.V. about graduating from college?") But, assuming those acts are *collateral*, that they have nothing to do with the case other than to show that the witness is a liar, you cannot present *extrinsic evidence* of those dishonest acts; you must accept the witness's answer, in the sense that you cannot put on any other evidence to show that the answer is not truthful. You can, however, press the witness, again within the court's discretion, and even attempt to "refresh" her memory by showing her documents that conflict with her testimony.

Now suppose that, after you have attacked the primary witness's character for truthfulness – perhaps by asking about those dishonest acts or by putting on a character witness – your opponent puts on a witness to testify to the primary witness's good character for truthfulness. You can, again in the discretion of the court, cross-examine this last witness as well about the primary witness's dishonest acts. If she did not know about them, or she did but they did not affect her assessment, that may well vitiate the force of her testimony. But again you must take the witness's answer.

> Similarly, a witness who testified to the primary witness's bad character for truthfulness could be cross-examined about honest acts that the primary witness committed.

This set of rules creates an odd dynamic. Not only is the cross-examiner not required to present evidence of the dishonest acts, other than the answers on cross themselves, but she is *not even allowed to*. So there may be a temptation to concoct some outlandish act and ask for confirmation of whether the witness committed it; an incredulous and outraged negative answer would not nullify the smear. The tactic would be blatantly improper – the cross-examiner must have a good-faith basis for asking the question – and, perhaps thanks to judicial vigilance and standards of professional conduct, it does not appear to be common.

3.   Prior convictions (FRE 609)

The rule against impeaching a witness by presenting affirmative evidence of a prior bad act has one great big exception: In nearly all jurisdictions, a witness's prior convictions for some crimes may be proven for impeachment. The basic idea behind this doctrine is that an exception is warranted in the case of a conviction for some crimes that are deemed highly probative of untruthfulness, given that a conviction is both relatively simple to prove and indicates to a high degree of confidence that the witness actually committed the crime. This is a very controversial topic, and the rules differ substantially from one jurisdiction to another. For simplicity, we will focus on FRE 609, with which rulemakers have tinkered over the years but which remains close to traditional doctrine. Under FRE 609, two general classes of prior convictions may be admitted for impeachment; we can refer to these in shorthand as *crimes of dishonesty* and *felonies*.

Crimes of dishonesty (FRE 609(a)(2))

If a witness has previously been convicted of a crime that involved dishonesty, that clearly may have some significance in assessing the probability that the witness is lying under oath now. The point should not be overstated. Many factors may explain why a witness would commit a crime of dishonesty on one occasion and yet adhere rigorously to the truth on another. But the past crime may reasonably affect the fact-finder's credibility determination. The rulemakers felt so strongly about this that they provided that a prior conviction meeting the criteria for a crime of dishonesty *must* be admitted. No other provision of the FRE mandates admission of an item of evidence. (Rule 609 also says felonies "must" be admitted, but only if a discretionary standard is satisfied.) And the mandate applies even if the evidence is offered against a criminal defendant – an outcome that I will question below.

What constitutes a crime of dishonesty? The category clearly includes crimes, such as perjury and forgery, the definition of which makes a dishonest act an essential element. Rule 609(a)(2) goes beyond these.

At the other extreme, one could include any crime the commission of which involved a dishonest act. For example, it may be that the witness was convicted of robbery after gaining access to a house by misidentifying himself. Rule 609(a)(2) does not go so far as to include such convictions. (The court still has discretion under FRE 608(b) to allow cross-examination of the witness on the basis of the misidentification, which in itself is a dishonest act.) But the Rule does include convictions in which, under the theory charged in the particular case, a dishonest act was an essential element, so long as the court can readily determine that fact. For example, dishonesty is not an essential element of obstruction of justice; one may obstruct justice by threatening a witness. But if in the given case the court can readily determine that the prosecution could have won a conviction only by proving that the then-accused (now the witness being impeached) lied to investigators to mislead them, then that conviction would qualify under Rule 609(a)(2). The Advisory Committee meant the ready-determination standard to allow the court to examine not only the statute under which the witness was charged in the prior proceeding but also the charging instrument, a plea agreement or colloquy during a plea hearing, or jury instructions, but not to hold "a 'mini-trial' in which the court plumbs the record of the previous proceeding."

Felonies (FRE 609(a)(1))

The other category designated by Rule 609 is crimes punishable by death or imprisonment for more than one year. (What matters is the maximum possible punishment for the offense, not the punishment actually imposed.) Rule 609(a)(1) creates a split standard for admission of these crimes. If the witness is anyone other than a criminal defendant in the case being tried, then the usual standard of FRE 403 applies; that is, the court should (or, in the language now favored by the Rules, must) admit the evidence unless its probative value for impeachment is substantially outweighed by the danger of prejudice and other negative factors. (FRE 609(a)(1)(A)) And if the witness is being tried criminally, the thumb is put on the other side of the scale: "[I]f the probative value of the evidence outweighs its prejudicial effect to that defendant," then and only then must the court admit it. (FRE 609(a)(1)(B))

Let's first consider whether admission of felonies for impeachment makes sense when the witness is someone other than a criminal defendant. Many felonies involve no dishonesty: A robber who sticks a gun in his victim's ribs and says "This is a stickup" is being brutally honest. Nevertheless, there is a correlation among various forms of antisocial behavior; indeed, that is what a diagnosis of antisocial personality disorder (ASPD) is all about. As a probabilistic matter, one who commits one serious form of antisocial behavior, a felony, is more likely to be willing to commit another, lying under oath, even though the first involved no dishonesty.

Now, assuming that admission of felonies for impeachment makes sense with respect to most witnesses, does the differential standard for criminal defendants make sense? I think the answer is definitely yes. In fact, I believe the differential is a rather minor move along a path that should be followed much further to the ultimate conclusion: A criminal defendant should not be subject to character impeachment evidence – not by convictions or in any other way – unless he introduces evidence of his good character.

Montana Rule of Evidence 609 flatly prohibits use of prior convictions to impeach the credibility of a witness. Hawaii's Rule 609 prohibits the use of convictions to impeach an accused unless he first presents evidence of his good character. In England and Wales, CJA 2003, s. 101 limits the circumstances in which evidence of an accused's bad character is admissible – and whether or not he chooses to testify has no direct bearing on the matter.

On one side of the ledger, character impeachment serves little purpose when the accused testifies in his own defense. His motivation to lie to save himself is already apparent. Moreover, in asking the key question in assessing his credibility – how likely would he testify to an exculpatory story if it were untrue? – the jury already assumes hypothetically that the accused committed the crime charged; conviction for a past crime is unlikely to have much incremental value. I've previously summarized this part of the argument by saying that for character impeachment evidence of an accused to have an impact on credibility, the jury would have to go through reasoning like this: "At first, I thought it was very unlikely that, if Defoe committed robbery, he would lie about it. But now that I know he committed forgery a year before, that possibility seems substantially more likely." And this thinking, I contend, utterly lacks logic or common sense. (*Character Impeachment Evidence: Psycho-Bayesian [!?] Analysis and a Proposed Overhaul*, UCLA L. Rev. (1991))

On the other side, the threat of character impeachment often imposes a prohibitive cost on the right of an accused with a prior conviction to testify in his own defense: It may be that if he testifies he will be hammered by proof of a conviction that would otherwise be inadmissible. And if he does testify and the conviction is admitted for impeachment, there is often a serious risk of prejudice: The jury is supposed to use the prior conviction only for impeachment, but, especially if the conviction is for a crime similar to the one presently charged, the temptation may be irresistible to draw the prohibited propensity inference that the accused, having committed the crime once before, is more likely to have done so again.

4.   Contradiction

If a witness testifies to a proposition, the adversary may obviously present contradictory evidence. And that contradiction may impeach the witness with respect not only to the given proposition but also to any other proposition as to which she has testified; if the jury loses faith in her credibility on one matter, that may carry over to other matters as well.

There is really only one substantial complexity with respect to impeachment by contradiction: The same rule against impeaching by extrinsic evidence on collateral matters that we have seen in the context of prior bad acts also applies in this context. That is, if the matter is deemed collateral – the contradiction has nothing to do with the case other than to show that the witness is a liar – then the impeaching party can only try to prove the contradiction out of the mouth of the witness herself. But if the matter is collateral, how did the witness come to testify about it? It could be simply that the opposing party failed to object, either intentionally or inadvertently. Or perhaps the witness's testimony on that proposition came out incidentally as part of a longer narrative on clearly material matters. Or it may be that the impeaching party laid a trap; knowing the witness would likely testify falsely on the given matter, the impeaching party may have tried to draw her out, in hopes that impeachment would make her look less credible.

Sometimes there are close questions as to whether a matter should be deemed collateral. How many alcoholic drinks a witness had before a crucial conversation should not be considered collateral, because it may have a bearing on her ability to observe and remember. Just what those drinks were should probably be deemed collateral absent evidence that the impact on her depends on the identity of the drink. Or consider the famous old case of *State v. Oswalt* (Washington 1963). Oswalt was accused of committing robbery in Seattle on July 14. One Ardiss testified that Oswalt was in Ardiss's restaurant in Portland on that date, which would give Oswalt an alibi. On cross-examination, Ardiss testified that Oswalt had been in his restaurant every day for a couple of months. The prosecution then presented the testimony of a police officer that he had seen Oswalt in Seattle on June 12, and that Oswalt said that he had been there for a couple of days. The state supreme court held this testimony should not have been admitted; where Oswalt was on June 12 was not a material issue. True enough. But what was the basis of Ardiss's professed belief that Oswalt was in his restaurant on July 14? If he had an independent memory of that date (maybe Oswalt sang at the Bastille Day celebration?) then the question of June 12 is indeed collateral. But if Ardiss only had an undifferentiated memory of a month's-long period, from which he inferred Oswalt's presence on July 14, then puncturing the major premise by demonstrating that Oswalt really was not there every night seems highly material. In any event, the bottom-line question is not whether the issue should be deemed collateral but whether the extrinsic evidence should be allowed, and an assessment of its significance is likely to be more important than categorical analysis.

5.   Prior inconsistent statements and other conduct (FRE 801(d)(1)(A), 613)

Contradiction can come in a particularly strong form – by a prior statement or other conduct of the witness herself. Thus, if a witness who has testified to a proposition X has previously asserted Not-X, then the fact of that inconsistency may be proved to impeach her credibility, even if the hearsay rule prevents the prior statement from being introduced to prove the truth of what it asserts. The logic can be captured in an aggressive form of cross-examination that is sometimes allowed: "Are you lying now or were you lying then?" Even if lying on one occasion or another is not the only plausible explanation of the inconsistency – perhaps, for example, the witness was forgetful on one occasion or the other – the fact that on a prior occasion the witness said something contrary to her current testimony may well undermine the jury's confidence in her testimony. Indeed, a logical inconsistency between the prior statement and the current testimony (such as X and Not-X) is not necessary for the doctrine to apply. It is enough that the prior statement be such that the witness is significantly less likely to have made it if she then believed the substance of the current testimony than if she didn't. Moreover, the doctrine easily extends to non-assertive conduct. If, for example, a witness testifies that the accused was at a meeting and the prior statement did not list the accused among the attendees, that would have impeachment value even though the prior statement did not clearly purport to provide an exhaustive list of attendees, so there is no logical incompatibility between the two statements. Or if a store owner testifies to how trustworthy and methodical her clerk was, the owner may be impeached by evidence that she carefully reconciled the cash and receipts at the end of each day on which the clerk worked. Or if a witness testifies that she was in the shower at a crucial time, evidence that she had just had a perm, which would be undone by showering too soon afterwards, may have devastating impeachment effect. (It certainly did in *Legally Blonde*.)

Now, what is the difference between admitting a prior statement to impeach and admitting it for the truth of what it asserts? Let's assume the prosecution is trying to prove the accused was at a meeting, and let's also suppose that the witness testifies that he wasn't but her prior statement asserted that he was. We might say that if the prior statement is admitted only for impeachment, then a juror can use it at most to nullify the effect of the witness's current testimony (with respect to any proposition, not just the one that is the subject of the witness's testimony), but not to assign to the proposition that the accused was at the meeting a higher probability than she would have assigned before the witness testified. But jurors might have a hard time limiting themselves in this way. The more significant difference, I believe, is that if a party has the burden of proving the proposition asserted by the prior statement, then admitting the statement only for impeachment will not help it satisfy that burden; if the prosecution has to prove that the accused was at the meeting, and it has no other evidence of that fact, then if the prior statement is admitted only for impeachment the case will not get to the jury.

But this factor is often overlooked, and so in recent decades there has been something of a tendency to minimize the difference between admitting a statement for impeachment and for its truth. California Evidence Code § 1235 generally removes the hearsay bar to a witness's prior inconsistent statement, and the Advisory Committee for the Federal Rules proposed following suit. Among the reasons given, as noted on p. 31, was the curious one that this rule provided protection against a turncoat witness who changed her testimony on the stand. Why, we might ask, is protecting a party (usually a prosecutor) against a witness who at trial disappoints the party a good thing? Isn't the possibility of such disappointment the essence of why we require oath and cross-examination? And so the House of Representatives opposed allowing substantive use of the statement unless the statement was made subject to oath and confirmation. The Senate restored the Advisory Committee proposal, and ultimately the two Houses adopted an odd compromise, allowing substantive use if the statement was made under penalty of perjury in a proceeding or deposition; thus, under FRE 801(d)(1)(A), if a witness's trial testimony is inconsistent with her grand jury testimony, then the earlier testimony can be introduced not only for impeachment but also for its truth.

As with impeachment by prior bad acts (other than convictions) and contradiction, impeachment by prior inconsistent statement cannot be made by extrinsic evidence if the matter is collateral. Thus, for example, if a witness to an accident testifies that she was on her way home from lunch with her friend Lucinda, an opposing party might impeach her on cross-examination by asking, "Didn't you previously tell Maria that you were on your way home from lunch with Roberta?," but he could not put Maria on the stand to testify to the prior conversation.

Traditional law prescribed a rigid procedure for impeachment by prior inconsistent statements. (And in England and Wales, Criminal Procedure Act 1865, ss. 4, 5 still do.) The impeaching party first had to draw the witness's attention to the time and circumstances of the statement, and then show her the statement, if it was in writing. Only then could the impeacher question the witness about the statement, and only after doing so could the impeacher offer extrinsic evidence of the statement (assuming it was not on a collateral matter). FRE 613 replaces this procedure by a much less restrictive one. The impeaching counsel can ask the witness about the prior statement without prior disclosure; on request, she must show the statement or disclose its contents to an adverse party's counsel. This part of Rule 613 effectively discards the old concern about surprising the witness. And extrinsic evidence of the statement may be introduced before the witness is examined about it, so long as she has a chance at some point to explain or deny it and the adverse party can examine it; this latter set of requirements does not apply to party admissions, or if for unusual circumstances (say, the impeacher only learned about the prior statement after the witness was excused and left the country) the interests of justice require flexibility.

Despite the clarity of the Rule, some federal courts still require questioning of the witness before the extrinsic evidence is offered. (Katherine T. Schaffzin, *Sweet Caroline: The Backslide from Federal Rule of Evidence 613(b) to the Rule in Queen Caroline's Case*, Mich. J. L. Ref. (2014).) And a proposed amendment to FRE 613 would restore this part of the traditional rule as a presumptive matter.

6.　　Bias

One of the most powerful methods of impeaching a witness is to demonstrate bias. In this context, bias of course includes like or dislike of a party, but it is much broader: It includes any factor that might deflect a witness from the obligation to tell the truth. Thus, suppose that an employee is testifying in an action in which her boss is a party. Even if she doesn't like the boss, the other party could well impeach on the basis of bias; she may have a strong interest in giving testimony that will please him.

Bias is not a matter of character. Rather, it is treated as a case-specific factor that interferes with the witness's ability to tell the truth. In this sense, demonstrating bias is comparable to demonstrating that the witness did not have an unobstructed ability to observe the events at issue. This means in effect that bias is not deemed to be collateral. On the contrary, it is treated as a part of the story by which the evidence has reached the state that it has – the jury has to decide whether that was by a route under which the facts are as the witness described them, truthfully, or by a route under which the witness's bias led her to give a false description. And the consequence of this is that bias may be proved like any material fact, brick by brick: Extrinsic evidence is permissible, and the party wishing to prove bias may (subject to the court's discretionary control) present evidence of particular incidents.

A criminal defendant's interest in demonstrating bias of witnesses against him is so strong that in some instances it is constitutionally protected under the Confrontation Clause. The key case is *Davis v. Alaska* (1974). Davis was accused of stealing a safe, which was found, door pried open, near Straight's property. Green, Straight's 16-year-old stepson, testified that he had seen Davis near the safe with something like a crowbar. Green was on probation, having been judged delinquent for burglarizing two cabins. State law generally prohibited use of such juvenile adjudications as evidence in other proceedings. But the Supreme Court held that Davis had a constitutional right to present evidence of Green's record, not to show that Green was likely the perpetrator but because the record might have made him realize that he would be an object of suspicion and so given him an incentive to cast the blame elsewhere.

7. Capacities other than truth-telling

We have focused principally on impeachment meant to make it appear more probable that the witness was speaking dishonestly. But a good deal of cross-examination, and impeachment generally, is directed at other capacities, mainly perception and memory. In large part, though the law with respect to these is less clearly developed, it seems to follow along the same lines as the law on truthfulness. Thus, a secondary witness could testify that the primary witness was not in a good position to observe the events or conditions on which she has testified. A secondary witness who is familiar with the primary witness will usually be able to give an overall assessment of the primary witness's general capacities of perception or memory. The primary witness can be cross-examined about her general capacities, and cross-examination about particular incidents suggesting a defect should be allowed, within the trial court's discretion. The court will usually be more leery of allowing extrinsic evidence of such incidents if they are collateral to the case. But if, say, a witness has given a detailed description of a material incident that happened in the distance, the court might be willing to allow a secondary witness to testify to another incident showing the primary witness has poor eyesight; eyesight runs truer to form than does honesty. This is an area very much within the trial court's discretion.

C. Rehabilitation (FRE 801(d)(1)(B))

If a witness has been impeached, then the party supporting her testimony – usually but not inevitably the party that called her to testify – may present evidence supporting her credibility. This *rehabilitation* usually takes one of two forms – character evidence or prior consistent statements. Which one is appropriate depends on how the witness has been impeached.

First, suppose the witness's character for truthfulness has been attacked. This occurs, of course, if the impeaching party presents a witness to testify to the primary witness's bad character for truthfulness. But the court could also deem that it occurs if the impeaching party cross-examines the primary witness about past dishonest acts, or proves that she had prior convictions, or asks about her hopes for leniency on a pending charge, or subjects her to a withering cross-examination that may suggest not only that the witness is lying in the particular case but that a character defect makes her more likely to do so. However the primary witness's character for truthfulness has been attacked, the supporting party may attempt to rehabilitate her by presenting a witness to offer opinion or reputation testimony that she had a good character for truthfulness. But take care! Such a witness, like the primary witness herself, may be impeached by asking her on cross about particular dishonest acts that the primary witness has committed.

Also, if the impeachment has been through a character witness, the supporting party may ask that witness about any particular incident suggesting that in fact the primary witness is a truthful person.

Now suppose that the primary witness has been impeached by a demonstration of bias. Perhaps the witness received an overly generous settlement payment from the defendant. Or perhaps her sister's marriage to the defendant dissolved in acrimony. In such cases, she may be rehabilitated by proof that, before the cause of bias arose, she made a statement consistent with her current testimony; that strongly suggests that the bias factor, however forceful it may be, does not account for the witness's testimony. If the prior consistent statement was made *after* the cause of bias arose, then it probably does not have much rehabilitative value; the bias could account for the prior statement just as easily as it could for the current testimony. Indeed, recall from pp. 32–33 that in *Tome v. United States* (1995) the Supreme Court – interpreting FRE 801(d)(1)(B), which provides for substantive use of certain prior consistent statements – announced a firm rule under which only statements made before the biasing motive would qualify. But, as I pointed out in that discussion, there may be some circumstances in which even a statement made after a biasing motive arose may have considerable rehabilitative value: The statement may appear to be so spontaneous that it is unlikely to have been the product of conscious distortion of the facts; the biasing motive may have arisen but not yet achieved the strength it had at trial; and the statement may have been made in circumstances, such as to a confidante, in which the witness would have no incentive to speak falsely.

Of course, sometimes the cause of bias has existed from before the time of the events or conditions on which the witness has reported – an adjuster for the defendant's insurance company was presumably biased from the start.

Finally, suppose that the witness has been impeached by a prior inconsistent statement or other conduct. Then proof that before that conduct she made a statement consistent with her trial testimony would have rehabilitative value. It would dispel the inference that some testimonial failure – perhaps an intervening motive or loss of memory? – after the time of the inconsistent conduct accounts for the trial testimony. It would still leave the proponent having to explain the inconsistency, but perhaps, given that before the inconsistent conduct the witness spoke consistently with the later trial testimony, the inconsistent statement or other conduct will appear to be the anomaly. Perhaps some factor peculiar to the circumstances that then prevailed can help explain it away. (Was she distracted? Was she speaking to a person to whom she did not then want to acknowledge the truth?)

If the witness made the prior consistent statement after the inconsistent conduct, it usually will not have significant rehabilitative value; the same testimonial failure could well explain both the prior consistent statement and the trial testimony. But there is no hard-and-fast line, at least if the inconsistent conduct was failure to speak when it would have been natural to. Consider *People v. Gentry* (Cal. Apps. 1969). Gentry was accused of injuring a small child with whom he was living. Turner, a friend of his who had been drinking with him and fallen asleep, testified that, while half awake, he heard a child crying, footsteps, and then a loud thud or slap. He was impeached by evidence that when he was first asked by an officer on the scene what he had heard or seen he failed to implicate Gentry. But Turner was groggy then – he had to be shaken to be awakened – and the prosecution was allowed to prove that later that morning he went to the sheriff's office where he made a statement consistent with his trial testimony. The appellate court held that this statement, made "at the earliest opportunity after he had recovered his senses," was valid rehabilitation.

16 Expert evidence (FRE 701-706)

An ordinary lay witness is allowed to testify because she has some information, from first-hand observation, that might be useful to the jury. Most often that information comes from having observed a particular event of significance to the action. But it could also be from personal observation of some condition, perhaps over an extended period. For example, it may be that, although the witness did not observe any event that in itself is material to the action, long familiarity enables her to identify a voice heard on a crucial recording. This witness has something in common with an expert witness: What she has to offer the jury is not personal observations on which the action centers, but knowledge, which the jury cannot be expected to have acquired, that she has acquired at different times and places. Such a witness would still be considered a lay witness, however, because recognizing the voices of people we know is something most of us do. An expert, by contrast, has knowledge of a type that most of us do not. Such knowledge could be the diagnostic criteria for a rare disease, or it could be that a given pair of tire marks must have been made by a car with positraction and independent rear suspension, which the 1964 Buick Skylark did not have but the 1963 Pontiac Tempest did. (If you haven't seen *My Cousin Vinny* already, just do it.) The complex subject of expert evidence is enormously important, because it plays a large and increasing role in modern litigation.

A. When is expert testimony allowed, and when is it required? (FRE 701, 702)

FRE 702(a) sets out a general standard for when expert testimony is appropriate, whether the expert has some form of "specialized knowledge" that "will help the trier of fact to understand the evidence or to determine a fact in issue." To be helpful, the expert has to have knowledge that the trier does not. We do not need an expert to tell the jury that being hit by a sledgehammer in the head may cause long-lasting headaches. But perceptions that are not so well understood may be helpful, and those that are counterintuitive (and yet well grounded) may be particularly useful. Thus, identification of a captive with her aggressor, behavior that might otherwise be difficult to fathom, may appear more comprehensible when an expert is able to testify that the "Stockholm syndrome" is a recognized psychological phenomenon by which a hostage develops positive feelings for her captor. Or a rape complainant's delay in reporting and lack of outward distress may be easier to understand as part of a common combination of responses known as rape-trauma syndrome. A tougher question is posed when a party seeks to have an expert testify about factors that might undermine an eyewitness's credibility. Some courts have resisted such expert testimony on the ground that it would usurp the role of the jury in determining the credibility of the witness. But recently the trend seems to be to recognize that on some questions – such as the weakness of correlation between a witness's accuracy and the confidence with which she delivers her testimony – an expert may have information that would not be obvious to the jury and that might help it in performing its functions.

In some circumstances, expert testimony is not only allowed but required. A witness who has no expertise on the subject could not testify, "In my opinion, the physician waited too long before performing a Caesarian." That would not satisfy FRE 701 as "helpful ... to determining a fact in issue," and so be a valid lay opinion, because the witness is in no better position than the jury to offer it. The more difficult question is whether the jury ought to be able to draw such a conclusion without expert advice. Sometimes, it appears the answer should be affirmative, because the breach of professional standards is so glaring. But in recent decades "tort reform" statutes in many states have required expert affidavits of merit at the beginning of litigation in certain types of cases, typically those claiming medical malpractice.

B.   The expert before trial: recruitment, reports, and discovery

Of course, all else equal, a party would almost always prefer to present an expert witness on a given issue. But it is not so easy. The precept that the law is entitled to every person's evidence applies to percipient witnesses

– those who happen to have been in position to observe an event or condition significant to the action – but not to experts who have no connection to the events at issue but whose background knowledge may be helpful in assessing the other evidence in the case. You may have to do considerable research to find a suitable expert whose testimony would be both helpful and persuasive. And then you have no guarantee you'll be able to secure her testimony. You can compel a percipient witness by subpoena to testify, and pay a nominal fee for her attendance. But you cannot compel an expert to testify. Persuasion might be difficult if you are asking her to criticize the work of her professional peers. And you will likely have to pay her a substantial fee.

Some experts are also percipient witnesses. Put another way, just because a person is a percipient witness (and subject to subpoena) does not preclude her from offering an expert opinion that she is qualified to give.

The fee in itself highlights a significant set of problems. An ordinary percipient witness can be compelled to testify to what she observed, and indeed she may not be paid for doing so beyond the modest statutorily prescribed fees. But an expert, not being compelled, effectively sells her participation. And though that participation may culminate in testimony from the witness stand, what she is really selling is presentation of an inference; thus, she is akin to an advocate making an argument. And she knows that if she wants to close the sale, she must be prepared to make an argument that you will find useful; indeed, most often, if you are an experienced lawyer with resources, you will, before making a formal overture, ascertain that the expert is on your side.

If you retain the expert in anticipation that she will testify at trial, you will probably have to disclose to your adversary (either as an initial matter or in response to discovery requests) the expert's identity, the subject matter on which she will testify, and a summary of the substance of her testimony. If you are in federal court, you will have to provide a fuller report by the expert that forecasts the testimony comprehensively and gives your adversary information, such as a list of publications and of other cases in which she has testified, that may lay the ground for impeachment – and after that your adversary may take the expert's deposition.

C. Reputability of the evidence (FRE 702)

Courts have long been concerned that misleading evidence presented through a professed expert might have an undue effect on the jury and so distort the fact-finding process. For many years, the dominant expression of this view in American courts was a statement in *Frye v. United States* (D.C. Ct. Apps. 1923):

> Just when a scientific principle or discovery crosses the line between the experimental and demonstrable stages is difficult to define. Somewhere in this twilight zone the evidential force of the principle must be recognized, and while courts will go a long way in admitting expert testimony deduced from a well-recognized scientific principle or discovery, the thing from which the deduction is made must be sufficiently established to have gained general acceptance in the particular field in which it belongs.

Nothing in the FRE suggested that they retained this "austere standard," as *Daubert v. Merrell Dow Pharmaceuticals, Inc.*, 509 U.S. 579, 589 (1993), characterized it, and the *Daubert* Court held unanimously that it was supplanted by the language of Rule 702, which emphasizes helpfulness to the fact-finder. Had the Court stopped there, *Daubert* would appear to have eased the admissibility of expert evidence; the decision reversed a judgment that had held inadmissible evidence that plaintiffs believed proved a link between the drug Bendectin and birth defects in humans. But seven justices went on to outline a "gatekeeping role" for the court in determining whether evidence offered as scientific (as was the evidence in *Daubert* itself) ought to be admitted (*Id.* at 597); the effort, the Court said, was necessary to ensure that scientific evidence would be "not only relevant, but reliable" (*Id.* at 589).

Criminal courts in England and Wales also make reliability a touchstone of admissibility for expert evidence. Note, for example, the guidance given in Part 19A of the Criminal Practice Directions.

Issued at a time of rising concern about the impact of "junk science," the decision has come to be regarded as reflecting skepticism about some assertedly scientific or other technical evidence. While recognizing that any approach must be flexible, Justice Blackmun's majority opinion laid out several criteria that would often enter into a decision.

1.   General acceptance

Let's begin with this factor (though Justice Blackmun put it last), because it is the essence of the *Frye* test, which still governs in some states. Although the *Daubert* majority declined to read *Frye* into the FRE, it still thought that general acceptance plays a role in determining admissibility. But the standard contains several ambiguities.

First, *what must be "generally accepted"*? If it is only the broad underlying theory, then the standard does not have much force; pretty much everyone agrees on the laws of physics, for example. If it is the particular application, then the test is probably too demanding, because even like-minded experts who respect each other might disagree as to how commonly held principles play out in a given case; moreover, if the question is sufficiently particular, it probably has not been studied enough to make determination of the level of acceptance feasible. Justice Blackmun addressed this issue briefly, saying that the focus must be on "principles and methodology, not on the conclusions they generate" (*Id.* at 595). But in the Court's first opportunity to expand on this distinction, in *General Electric Co. v. Joiner* (1997), it instead stepped away from it. The plaintiffs there argued that, in excluding evidence by their toxicologist experts as to a link between a set of chemicals and cancer, the trial court had rejected their conclusions rather than their methodology. "But conclusions and methodology are not entirely distinct from one another," wrote Chief Justice Rehnquist (one of the two members of the Court who had not joined all of *Daubert*) for the Court (522 U.S. at 146).

Second, *how broad is the relevant community* in which acceptance is measured? If the community is defined as those who practice a given technique, then the test would allow evidence based on fringe theories; the community of phrenologists unanimously supports the principle of phrenology. The problem is particularly significant because some techniques are practiced principally by forensic scientists, who testify mainly for prosecutors.

Third, *how unanimous* must acceptance be? Some courts have treated the inquiry rigorously, so that if there appears to be a reputable body of persons in the field who disagree with a given view it cannot be deemed "to have gained general acceptance." (*Frye v. United States*, 293 F. 1013, 1014 (D.C. Cir. 1923)) Such an approach would eliminate the so-called battle of the experts, keeping theoretical disputes from being played out in front of the jury, but it would be extremely restrictive, often denying the fact-finding process of valuable information. (Note *Atkins and Atkins v. R.* (Eng. & W. Ct. App. Crim Div. 2009), expressing a similar concern about an overly rigorous standard.) *Daubert* indicates receptivity to a more lenient approach; it uses the term "[w]idespread acceptance" as an alternative formulation (509 U.S. at 594), and this seems preferable.

Fourth, *how must acceptance be demonstrated?* Some courts have allowed the expert herself to testify that her approach has gained general acceptance; at the other pole, an occasional court might demand "independently conducted validation tests and control studies." (*People v. Young* (Mich. 1986))

2. Testing

Another criterion raised by Justice Blackmun was whether the theory or technique "can be (and has been) tested." (*Daubert*, 509 U.S. at 593) The "can be" refers to the concept of falsifiability, which is a, or arguably the, hallmark of scientific inquiry. A proposition is falsifiable if a test can be devised such that, assuming hypothetically that the proposition is false, the test will reveal it to be so. But suppose the litigation deals with a relatively new situation – say, the effects of a chemical that has not been studied over decades – and the plaintiff presents an expert's testimony that, putting together disparate bits of information in the light of her long experience, she believes the chemical is carcinogenic. (That's essentially what happened in *Joiner*.) That inference has not been tested, and it may not even be falsifiable. Perhaps that means that it is not scientific. But does that mean the expert's opinion is not worthy of being heard and considered by the fact-finder?

3. Peer review and publication

Justice Blackmun also emphasized "whether the theory or technique has been subjected to peer review and publication." (*Id.*) Certainly that can be a significant consideration, but peer review and publication are very imperfect screens, and in the modern age many scientific papers are circulated informally and well understood long before publication. Moreover, again as in *Joiner*, a litigated issue may be too new or too particularized to have generated peer-reviewed publications.

4. Error rates, and standards

Focusing on techniques, Justice Blackmun mentioned the "known or potential rate of error" and "the existence and maintenance of standards controlling the technique's operation." (*Id.*) Once again, it is easy to see the appeal of these factors. But even a technique with a substantial degree of error can be useful evidence, if the error rate is known tolerably well. After all, even eyewitness testimony subject to oath and cross-examination – which I have called the gold standard of acceptable testimony, see p. 11 – is subject to a high (and not precisely determinable) rate of error. And as for operating standards, they are often a matter of intense debate within a field; often it is better to play out the debate in front of the jurors rather than prevent them from receiving potentially useful information.

5. The amended FRE – and an alternative approach

The *Daubert* criteria were not presented as a required checklist, though some courts have used them that way. And they seem more geared to determining whether a given theory is scientific than whether it can form the basis of good evidence; it is important to bear in mind that FRE 702 speaks of "scientific, technical or other specialized knowledge" under-lying expert evidence. Nevertheless, some courts have used the criteria even in cases where the evidence was not presented as scientific, and in *Kumho Tire Co., Ltd. v. Carmichael* (1999), holding that the trial court had acted properly in rejecting the testimony of a tire expert on the causes of a blowout, the Supreme Court encouraged the practice. Soon after the *Kumho* decision, in 2000, FRE 702 was amended to incorporate the basic approach of *Daubert*, with its emphasis on the reliability of expert evi-dence. The Rule now requires that the testimony be "based on sufficient facts or data" and "the product of reliable principles and methods," and that the expert's opinion "reflects a reliable application of the principles and methods to the facts of the case." The Advisory Committee empha-sized that the *Daubert* criteria are not always all appropriate to consider, and that in some circumstances others (such as "[w]hether the expert has unjustifiably extrapolated from an accepted premise to an unfounded conclusion") are; the *Daubert* criteria continue to get heavy judicial use, however.

My own view is that, at least in civil cases, courts have been overly strin-gent on *admissibility* of *individual items* of expert evidence and not willing enough to hold that a *body* of admissible evidence is *insufficient* to prove a proposition even if it includes expert testimony asserting that proposition. It is notable that in each of the three cases of the so-called *Daubert* trilogy – *Daubert* itself, *Joiner*, and *Kumho* – the question of admissibility arose in the context of a summary judgment motion by a civil defendant. In each case, the trial court held that expert evidence offered by the plaintiff in response to that motion would not be admissible, and that absent that evidence the plaintiffs did not have a viable case. But suppose that in each of these cases the court had reached the same conclusion even on the assumption that the expert evidence was admissible. That might seem strange at first, because usually if a plaintiff introduces admissible testimony asserting a given proposition X, the court cannot grant judgment as a matter of law on the basis that X is insufficiently proven. But expert evidence is different. What is at stake is not merely the accuracy of a witness's report of observations, which a jury is free to accept even if the court thinks it is probably false; rather, the expert is offering an inference and an explanation for it. And it seems perfectly appropriate for the court to say that a given piece of expert evidence is sufficiently helpful that it should be heard by the jury, assuming that the case gets that far, but that looking at the evidence as a whole there is not enough to get there. Such an approach better reflects the type of judgment a court should make. The attempt to limit expert evidence to that which a court deems "reliable" is misbegotten; a reliable process (as I believe American courts use the term) is one that is highly unlikely to yield a given result if that result is incorrect, and if we attempted to allow only reliable expert evidence then disputes involving expertise would virtually all be resolved by the court rather than before the jury. The testimony of the experienced toxicologist in *Joiner* that the chemicals there were capable of causing cancer was the type of evidence that the jury should hear, *assuming* the case was strong enough overall to reach the jury.

D.   The expert on the witness stand (FRE 703–705)

Even assuming that the subject matter of an expert's testimony would satisfy whatever standard of reputability the court applies, before a witness can testify as to an expert opinion the court must determine that she personally is qualified to give it. Because this is a decision for the judge, she must hear evidence for and against the expert's qualifications before making a determination. (By contrast, recall that the court need not decide whether it believes a lay witness has personal knowledge of the subject of her testimony; it need only determine that there is sufficient evidence for the jury to find that proposition, and so contrary evidence can be presented later.) This hearing, often called a *voir dire*, could be held out of the presence of the jury. But usually if the proposed testimony is going to be ruled inadmissible, it will happen before she takes the witness stand; if she does take the stand, therefore, it will appear highly likely that she will be deemed qualified. So while in form the hearing is held so that the court can determine whether the witness should be allowed to testify, really what is happening is that both sides are trying to persuade the trier of fact on the question of how much weight to give her opinion.

Now, assuming the expert is not a percipient one, she has no case-specific personal observations to offer the jury. It may be that she is asked to give an opinion on a general proposition, without herself tying it to the facts of the case. But most often, the proponent wants her to offer an opinion about the particular case. Traditionally, the concern about experts usurping the role of the jury played out in a rule preventing an expert from offering an opinion on an "ultimate issue" that the jury had to determine. The rule created frustration and required fine distinctions. FRE 704 did away with it. Thus, a medical expert can offer testimony that the physician-defendant failed to exercise due medical care in conducting an operation. Abrogation of the rule did not, however, entirely eliminate the need to make delicate distinctions. The Advisory Committee indicated that, under general principles, "opinions phrased in terms of inadequately explored legal criteria" – such as "Did T have capacity to make a will?" – should still be excluded. But "Did T have sufficient mental capacity to know the nature and extent of his property and the natural objects of his bounty and to formulate a rational scheme of distribution?" would pass muster.

After a would-be assassin of President Reagan was found not guilty by reason of insanity, a verdict widely condemned, Congress restored the ultimate-issue rule in part. FRE 704(b), added in 1984, bars an expert witness in a criminal case from stating "an opinion about whether the defendant did or did not have a mental state or condition that constitutes an element of the crime charged or of a defense." Although Congress's focus was on the insanity defense, the symmetry of the Rule means that it constrains prosecutors as well as defendants. And once again courts must draw narrow distinctions; the Rule does not prevent an expert from testifying as to the symptoms of a given mental disease and whether the accused had it. Very few states have adopted counterparts to this partial restoration of the ultimate-issue rule.

Though the rule has fallen out of favor, I believe that in some settings it reflects a valid underlying concern. The expert presumably does not know all the material facts of the case. Accordingly, a flat assertion, "The defendant did X," or "The plaintiff suffered Y," often involves the expert making implicit assumptions that lie beyond her expertise and that are on matters that the jury must determine. Often, her testimony should be in the form "Factual set F would be far more probable under account A than under Not-A." For example, a non-percipient witness should not testify, "The complainant was raped." But she could testify, "The symptoms exhibited by the complainant would be far more likely to appear if she were raped than if she were not."

> You might recognize that this would in effect be testifying in terms of the likelihood ratio.

Now, if that is the form in which the expert testifies, how does the witness learn factual set F? Perhaps she observed some of those facts – if, for example, she is a physician who, for the purpose of testifying about the medical condition of a person, has examined the person. Perhaps she has sat in on trial and assumes the truth of some of the testimony she has heard. But under traditional practice, to the extent these methods have not given her the facts necessary to render an opinion, she would have to be asked a hypothetical question. Such a question asks the expert to render an opinion assuming the truth of a set of facts laid out by the proponent. If the proponent, whether beforehand or subsequently, presents sufficient evidence of each of those predicate facts, then the linkage is made and the proponent can ask the fact-finder to accept those facts and the expert's opinion. This is all very logical. But it creates problems as well. Some lawyers use the opportunity to make what is effectively an extended, and premature, jury argument; no other type of question is likely to have to be suspended in the middle for the lunch hour! If the hypothetical is too skimpy, the expert might not be able to give an opinion, or she will be subject to impeachment for giving an insufficiently careful and nuanced one. If the hypothetical is too full, there may be difficulties in determining whether the proponent has in fact provided support for each of the essential predicates of the opinion.

FRE 705 altered the traditional practice by making the hypothetical question optional: "Unless the court orders otherwise, an expert may state an opinion – and give the reasons for it – without first testifying to the underlying facts or data"; an adversary may require the expert to disclose the facts or data on cross-examination.

Moreover, FRE 703 loosened the traditional requirement that the opinion be based on facts that at one point or another are proven at trial. The Rule says that the expert "may base an opinion on facts or data in the case that the expert has been made aware of or personally observed." No surprise there. But then the Rule provides that the opinion may be admitted if "experts in the particular field would reasonably rely on those kinds of facts or data in forming an opinion on the subject" – even if those predicate facts or data are themselves inadmissible. The reasoning behind this provision was that in their ordinary work experts frequently rely on outside sources of information – say, a physician relying on lab reports – and if those sources are good enough to support real-world decisions with life-and-death consequences, they ought to be good enough for fact-finding in court.

In most settings, this reasoning makes sense; Rule 703 streamlines the proof process. But notice that, assuming for the moment that the expert is allowed not only to *base her opinion* on the otherwise inadmissible material but also to *testify to* that material, this provision operates as a way around the hearsay rule and, in some cases, the confrontation right. How is that? The expert says she relied on a given piece of information in forming her opinion, and the information is admitted supposedly to show the basis for the opinion; but given that the information supports the opinion only if it is true, there is really no difference between doing this and admitting the information for its truth. In most settings, that may be all to the good – I'll repeat my view that it's beneficial to loosen up on the rule against hearsay when testimonial statements are not involved. But if the expert is testifying against a criminal defendant and forms her opinion in part by relying on a testimonial statement, then admitting that statement supposedly in support of her opinion should be considered a violation of the confrontation right. The court saw it that way in *People v. Goldstein* (N.Y. 2005), involving statements made to a forensic psychiatrist by persons who knew that she was investigating a widely publicized homicide. And five justices saw it that way in *Williams v. Illinois* (2012), though the latter was not a holding because, as discussed above on pp. 18–19, another set of five justices thought the lab report involved there was not testimonial.

> I have some of the same concern even if the testimonial statement is not itself admitted but the expert bases her opinion on it; the opinion may be in effect a way of repackaging the information in that statement and conveying it to the jury in a subtle form. But I may be idiosyncratic in that view. The pending case of *Smith v. Arizona* may lend some clarity to this area – or not.

In any event, in 2000 the rulemakers incorporated into FRE 703 a mild restriction on the ability of the expert's opinion to drag into evidence otherwise inadmissible information: The proponent may cause this result only if the information satisfies a balancing test that is essentially FRE 403 in reverse, with the probative value substantially outweighing the prejudicial effect. This provision imposes no limitation on the opponent, who may want to bring out that information if it seems to undercut the expert's opinion. And because it is written in loose terms, it does very little to protect the confrontation concern; as in other contexts, the confrontation right will have to stand on its own footing and not be supported by ordinary evidentiary law.

> Other similar reverse-403 balancing tests are contained in FRE 412 (rape shield) and 609 (prior convictions); see Chapters 12 and 15.

E.   Court-appointed experts (FRE 706)

By now, if not from the start, you may be wondering why American (and other common-law) courts put up with such an adversarially based system for securing expert guidance. Why not rely on neutral, court-appointed experts – which are explicitly authorized by FRE 706? In some recurrent contexts, such as child-custody cases, courts do tend to do this, and occasionally they do this in other litigation as well. But it isn't so easy.

> Why in child custody and not most other recurrent contexts, such as auto negligence? My colleague Sam Gross offers some possible explanations: Child-custody cases are tried without juries; courts want experts to tell them what to do; the parties may be unable to afford expertise; and state agencies often have it close at hand.

It takes time, as noted earlier, to determine who would be a suitable expert and then to select and recruit one. And in a system that is fundamentally adversarially oriented as a general matter, it is the parties and not the court that have the resources and incentive to perform these tasks. Moreover, even if the court does pick an expert, that is not the end of the story; the parties are entitled not only to cross-examine her (FRE 706(b)(4)), but also to put on experts of their own choice (FRE 706(e)). Lawyers used to controlling the presentation of their cases will not passively accept the testimony of a court-appointed expert whose testimony is unhelpful to them. So instead of reducing the number of experts from two to one, the court's appointment might increase the number to three.

> Court-appointed experts, like others, must be paid. FRE 706(c) allows the court to allocate the expense among the parties in a civil case.

Moreover, even in principle, it is not clear that court-appointment is a superior system. Lawyers in civil-law countries are sometimes dissatisfied that their system, dependent on court appointment, effectively delegates power to the scientific establishment with very little check. And the concept of neutrality is often elusive. Although the fact that an expert is appointed by the court suggests that she will not be motivated to help one party or the other, her testimony will still be guided by her own intellectual predilections, and there is no guarantee that she has a better key to truth than do party-selected experts.

> All that having been said, since 1998 English law has put significant pressure on the parties in most civil cases to agree on a single joint expert. There has not been much momentum in the United States towards adoption of a similar system. In Australia and some other ju-

risdictions, an alternative process known as "hot-tubbing" has taken hold; the respective experts meet and write a joint report, noting areas of agreement and disagreement; at trial, they testify simultaneously, in an interactive process.

Sam Gross has offered a couple of clever and intriguing suggestions of hybrid systems that could possibly improve the presentation of expert evidence. (Samuel R. Gross, *Expert Evidence*, Wisc. L. Rev. 1991) Under one, to testify as an expert, a witness must be court-appointed, but the court must appoint any qualified and willing expert who is designated by a party; the witness must not have been employed or received information bearing on the case from the designating party or anyone with similar interests. Any party or his representatives may communicate with an appointed expert, but the communications must be available to all sides. It is not hard to perceive reasons why this plan would not be accepted or wouldn't work, but it would have a chance, because it would keep the burden of initiative on the parties and yet, as compared to the current system, make the expert more of a disinterested witness and less of an advocate.

17 Structural and procedural considerations (FRE 103, 104, 106, 201, 301, 611, 901, 902, 1001-1008)

This chapter discusses a range of issues concerning such matters as the roles of judge and jury on preliminary questions, how evidence is presented, how the record is preserved, judicial notice, and burdens of proof.

A.   Preliminary questions: roles of judge and jury (FRE 103(d), 104)

Whether evidence A should be admitted will inevitably depend on some set of facts B. Let's compare two paradigmatic situations.

In situation 1, the plaintiff offers testimony of a witness W of a statement made by out-of-court declarant D describing an accident. So the evidence A is the statement, and let's suppose that it is not admissible unless it fits within the hearsay exception for excited utterances, which depends on B, the proposition that D was acting under the stress of the excitement of the accident when she made the statement.

In situation 2, Tenant wishes to prove that she gave timely notice to Landlord of her intent to renew a lease. She presents a letter, which was undisputedly received by Landlord, stating that intent. That is A. But the evidence is worthless unless fact B is true, that the letter was received on time.

The court should handle these two situations in very different ways, which stand out most clearly if we assume the trial is to a jury. In situation 1, it is the court's job to determine whether B is true. As FRE 104(a) says, "[t]he court must decide any preliminary question about whether ... evidence is admissible." It makes sense that this should be the judge's job;

it would not work well if the court had to instruct the jury, in effect, "You decide whether this statement was made while D was under the stress of excitement caused by the accident, and if you conclude that she wasn't, disregard it [even though it may be very persuasive]."

But a judge in England or Wales might have to give an instruction in much this form if a confession is alleged to have been obtained by oppression. (*R v. Mushtaq* (H.L. 2005)) Perhaps it is easier for jurors to follow such an instruction in that context, where the policy behind the exclusionary rule will be apparent to them.

Ordinarily, then, a court in situation 1 would decide whether B is *more likely true than not*, a standard that American courts tend to describe with the ill-fitting phrase *preponderance of the evidence* and that other courts describe by the apter phrase *balance of probabilities*. In making that determination, FRE 104(a) prescribes that "the court is not bound by evidence rules, except those on privilege." We can easily see the reason for this leeway: If in deciding B, the court were limited to using admissible evidence, then the court would face preliminary questions on *that* evidence, and then it would be limited to admissible evidence in resolving those questions, and so forth. This rule does mean giving way on whatever evidentiary policies – other than privileges and any that are based on a jury being the trier of fact – that would otherwise require exclusion, but balances of competing considerations are pervasive throughout evidentiary law.

Furthermore, the court has to do its best to avoid the jury hearing inadmissible evidence, or even suggestions of it. (FRE 103(d)) Accordingly, if there is any serious possibility that ultimately the court will hold A inadmissible, it ordinarily must determine whether B is true before deciding on the admissibility of A, and it must hear the evidence *for and against* B and make its decision at a side hearing, out of the presence of the jury.

Now compare situation 2. This is an example of what is commonly called *conditional relevance*. To put the matter simply, evidence A simply doesn't have enough to do with the case to warrant admissibility unless B is true, and let's assume there is no other reason to exclude A. Here, it's important for the jury to determine whether B is true, because it's part of the story that Tenant is trying to tell: "I sent Landlord a notice of intent to renew, *and she got it on time.*" It would be improper for the judge to rule, "I'm not going to let the jurors hear about the notice, because even though they might reasonably conclude that Landlord got it in time I don't believe he did."

And yet the court still has a role in situation 2, as FRE 104(b) indicates: It must determine whether the jury *could* reasonably find B to be true. And because B is part of the story the jury is determining, the evidence supporting B has to be admissible. Accordingly, the evidence supporting B is presented to the jury like any other evidence.

What's more, if B hasn't yet been supported, the court can admit A *subject to* B being proven later; the proponent sometimes promises the court, "I'll link things up." One reason this possibility is allowed is that there's not much downside: If in the end the jury does not find B to be true, then there wouldn't be much harm in the jury having heard evidence A, because A just wouldn't have much to do with the case, so presumably the jury would disregard it. And sometimes it is more convenient to prove one proposition before another even if that does not appear to be a logical order. But perhaps most often there is no order that is more logical than another, because A and B are each relevant conditionally on the other.

Suppose, for example, a prosecutor is trying to prove that a particular firearm was the weapon used to commit the murder being tried. Evidence that bullets fired with that gun would produce striations fitting a given pattern would not have much probative value on its own; nor would evidence that the bullet that killed the victim bore striations of that pattern. But together these two pieces of evidence are obviously extremely powerful – and there is no principle demanding that one or the other come first.

> Old joke: Mother gives Son two shirts. Next morning, Son comes downstairs wearing the blue one. Mother: "So, you didn't like the green one?" If you can't do two things at once, one or the other has to come first!

B.   Presenting testimony (FRE 611)

The party who calls a witness to the stand – the proponent – questions her first, on *direct* examination (or *examination-in chief*). The other side (or sides) then have an opportunity for *cross-examination*. There may then be *redirect* (or *re-examination)* and, in an American court, *recross*; rarely does the turn-taking extend beyond that.

There are various constraints on how questions are asked. For example, courts might reject a question if it is *vague*. If the vagueness of the question will not lead to uncertainty as to what the answer means – say, "Please describe the scene" – the court might just say, "The witness can answer if she understands the question." The court is more likely to reject a question if it is not certain just what is being asked ("Which is the best work site in your company?"). Similarly, the court will be disposed not to allow a *compound question,* two or more questions rolled into one ("Was he driving safely or over the speed limit?"), because it may not be clear what the answer means. A question that appears to ask the witness to draw a conclusion that the witness is not in a position to reach, or that the jury could reach just as well, may be rejected as *argumentative*; it may be *badgering* if the witness is hostile, but even if not, a question may be deemed argumentative if it is essentially an attempt to make the party's argument rather than seek information from the witness. At some point, if the questions appear to be replowing old ground, the court might rule *asked and answered.* Sometimes a question *assumes a fact not in evidence*: Note the three implicit premises in the question "When did you stop beating your spouse?" If any of them has not been established, the question would be improper.

Occasionally, particularly on direct, a court might hold that an open-ended question is too *narrative;* courts like the questioning lawyer to exercise some control so that the witness is less likely to veer off into prejudicial matter that is irrelevant or otherwise inadmissible. But probably the most common procedural constraint on direct examination points in the opposite direction: Ordinarily the proponent cannot ask *leading questions.* (FRE 611(c)) A leading question is one that, taking together all factors (language, context, tone), suggests the answer that the questioner desires. If, for example, the questioner states a proposition and asks for confirmation that it is true, that would probably be a very leading question. (Leadingness is a matter of degree.) If it appears that the questioner would be far more likely to ask a question as she did if she expected one answer than if she didn't, then the question would probably be considered leading.

Why shouldn't leading questions generally be allowed on direct? (Note that this is *not* a leading question.) They essentially take away from the witness's function; instead of being asked to remember what she observed and articulate a truthful answer, she is reduced to consenting to what are in effect assertions by the questioner. This makes the testimony far less persuasive, which raises the question of why the matter should not be self-regulated; ordinarily, a lawyer would not *want* to ask her own witness leading questions. Perhaps part of the answer is paternalistic, to protect parties against bad lawyering. But probably the best explanation is that the constraint is an example of the best-evidence principle: It may be that the questioner asks leading questions because she is trying to obscure the witness's weakness. From the point of view of the court, it is better to see how the witness can do without being propped up rather than having to guess, so excluding the leading questions will induce the presentation of a better form of evidence. And yet, in certain situations, leading questions on direct are allowed. Courts tend to tolerate them more when they are posed to child witnesses. They can be an efficient way of getting through uncontested matters, shifting topics, or focusing the witness's attention on a particular time or incident. They may also be used to refresh the memory of a forgetful witness, though the judge might want counsel to ask permission first. And if the witness has interests hostile to those of the party who put her on the stand – an adverse party necessarily fits this description – the court should allow leading questions.

That is because leading questions ordinarily are perfectly permissible on cross. (FRE 611(c)) Indeed, a good cross-examination will usually consist almost entirely of leading questions; styles differ from one jurisdiction to another, but American lawyers sometimes say, with only mild hyperbole, that the only answers on cross should be "yes" and "no." If leading questions were not allowed on cross, it would be far more difficult for the examiner to probe; the witness could answer vaguely or wander in directions that she preferred. But by asking leading questions, a cross-examiner can compel the witness to affirm or deny a given proposition; instead of asking "Where were you while this was going on?," she can ask, "You left the room at the first sign of trouble, didn't you?" Often, the cross-examiner begins by focusing on a given proposition to which the witness testified on direct, and then brings out information that makes that proposition less likely; sometimes a series of questions takes the form "You just testified that ... ," "But didn't you previously say that ...," which may sometimes culminate with the dramatic "Are you lying now or were you lying then?"

Jurisdictions have long divided over the question of how broad the permissible scope of cross-examination is. Some jurisdictions allow cross on any issue material to the case. Others say that cross is restricted, as FRE 611(b) puts it, to "the subject matter of the direct examination and matters affecting the witness's credibility." In the most rigorous form of this view, probably influenced by the fact that cross is itself an interruption in the proponent's presentation of its case, if the cross-examining party wants to explore other matters with the witness, he must wait until it is his turn to present evidence and then call the witness back to the stand (if that is possible). Not only is such a requirement inefficient, but few parties exercise the option; one can ask a few extra questions of a hostile witness without much risk, but if you call such a witness back to the stand you are raising juror expectations that something dramatic will happen. FRE 611(b) adopts a milder form of the restrictive approach: Presumptively, cross-examination should not go beyond the scope of the direct and matters affecting credibility (such as prior dishonest acts and matters suggesting bias). But the court may allow inquiry into additional matters "as if on direct examination," which ordinarily means that the examiner may not use leading questions. This resolution allows efficient presentation of testimony, without the cost of permitting a party whose adversary had to put him on the stand for a narrow purpose to be asked leading questions by his own lawyer on other parts of the case. Note also: A witness who testifies on a given subject cannot decline to answer questions on cross-examination on that subject, but she may assert the privilege against self-incrimination on another subject.

Redirect examination is not meant to be a second chance to ask questions the lawyer forgot to ask on direct; rather, it should address matters that arose on cross. Redirect can be a useful opportunity to mitigate the impact of an effective cross-examination, but it also poses dangers: the lawyer may not be confident what the witness's answer is, and the witness may not know whether the lawyer is hoping she will emphasize that the glass is half full or that it is half empty.

C. Presenting other forms of evidence (FRE 106, 901, 902, 1001–1008)

1. Real, demonstrative, and experimental evidence

Not all evidence is testimony. Sometimes a party shows a jury some image or tangible object or process. All such evidence is sometimes referred to as *demonstrative*, but it has become common, and it is useful, to use the term in a narrower sense, in contradistinction to *real* evidence – and I believe there is a third distinct category of non-testimonial evidence, which can be labeled *experimental*. Each of these three types of evidence has a different predicate for admission.

To qualify an item as *real evidence*, the proponent must present evidence that it actually played a role in the story being told. It could have been a cause of the litigated events – "*This* is the very weapon that the accused used to kill the victim" – but that is not necessary. It could be that the item was *created by* those events. Thus, if the accused is charged with robbing an automated teller machine at night, the recording that purports to show him in the act would be real evidence, and to get it admitted the prosecution would have to demonstrate how it came to exist and be presented in court – the placement and operation of the camera, and how the recording was maintained and transmitted.

Demonstrative evidence, by contrast, is an aid to a witness's testimony. Rather than simply describing the arrangement of objects at a crime scene, a witness might be able to testify, "This diagram is a fair and accurate representation of where everything was placed." It is not necessary that the witness testify to how the diagram came to be created, or that she had any role in its creation; indeed, it could have been created by counsel for the very purpose of aiding the witness's testimony.

Experimental evidence subjects a person or thing to a given stimulus so that the response can be assessed. If the experiment is sufficiently similar in material respects to the reality of the litigated events, then it might indicate something significant about those events. In O.J. Simpson's criminal trial, the prosecution tried an experiment, but it backfired badly: It asked Simpson to try on a glove that was allegedly found at the murder scene, but the glove did not fit and Simpson was ultimately acquitted.

In some accident litigation, parties present an *animation*. This is a form of demonstrative evidence, an attempt to illustrate with moving images the testimony of a witness (whether an eyewitness or an expert) as to how the accident occurred. There is no need to prove how the animation was created. Contrast a *simulation*. A computer program subjects data concerning the accident and surrounding conditions to a previously created computer model that, applying the material laws of physics, fills in the picture of how the accident occurred. This is a form of experimental evidence; the proponent's contention is that the model replicates reality by applying the laws of nature to accurate data.

2.   Authentication (FRE 901, 902)

The general principle running through each of the contexts just discussed is that non-testimonial evidence must be *authenticated* – that is, the proponent must introduce evidence that the item is what the proponent contends it is. The proponent cannot simply say, "Here is a letter that the defendant wrote." It must present evidence that the document is in fact a letter that the defendant wrote, and the mere fact that the document bears what purports to be the signature of the defendant is not enough. Authentication is a species of conditional relevance; if the item is not what the proponent contends it is, it probably has nothing to do with the case, but if the jury believes the item is what the proponent contends and there is no other reason to exclude it, then the jury ought to be able to consider it. Accordingly, the proponent need not satisfy the court that the item is what it contends; it need only, in the words of FRE 901, "produce evidence sufficient to support a finding" on the point. That is, it must present enough evidence that a fact-finder *could* make that finding. Rule 901 provides a non-exhaustive list of methods by which an item of evidence may be authenticated. The simplest, perhaps, is the testimony of a witness with knowledge that the item is what the proponent contends it is. Also, someone who does not know the particular document may testify that she recognizes the defendant's signature. A particularly interesting method pertains to what are often called ancient documents, though they only have to be 20 years old; if such a document "is in a condition that creates no suspicion as to its authenticity" (FRE 901(8)(A)), and it "was in a place where, if authentic, it would likely be" (FRE 901(8)(B)), that is enough for authentication. One might well ask whether these last two requirements should be sufficient without meeting a rather arbitrary age test. A document does not become more authentic with age – but older documents are likely to have been created before the litigation and therefore less likely to be suspicious, and arguably lack of suspiciousness should be enough whether or not age is a factor dispelling the concern.

Notwithstanding the general requirement of authentication, some documents are deemed *self-authenticating*; that is, no extrinsic evidence need be admitted to prove that they are what they appear to be. The origin of the concept of self-authentication appears to lie in official seals. The seal represents an official imprimatur that the document is what it appears to be, and courts have long given it respect. Public documents that are signed and sealed are now the first entry on the list of self-authenticating documents laid out by FRE 902. This is a closed list, not a non-exhaustive list of examples like FRE 901. In some cases an official's certification will suffice in place of an old-fashioned seal, and official publications issued by a public authority qualify as well. Newspapers and other periodicals are also on the list, among other documents the authenticity of which is rarely in doubt. An amendment in 2000 added a pair of provisions for certified records of regularly conducted activities. The effect of these is to allow a proponent to demonstrate that a document satisfies the hearsay exception for such activities (FRE 803(6)) without the need to produce a live witness. Another pair of provisions added in 2017 allows a similar certification process for electronically stored data and for records generated by an electronic process or system. It is arguable that these latter-day certification provisions, when invoked by a prosecutor, violate the Confrontation Clause, because the certification is itself clearly a statement that is made for use against an accused and is being used for the truth of what it asserts. But perhaps they should be considered comparable to seals, which as guarantors of the authenticity of a document have never been deemed to pose a confrontation problem.

3.   Completeness (FRE 106)

Cross-examination is an interruption in a party's case. Another is provided by the rule of completeness, which is expressed in FRE 106: If you present part of a statement or a series of statements, and that gives a misleading impression of the whole, then the other side is allowed at that time to introduce other portions that in fairness ought to be considered with it. But this *timing* function is only part of the effect of the rule of completeness, as Professor Dale Nance has pointed out: Sometimes it also performs a *trumping* function, overcoming what would otherwise be a bar to admissibility. *Beech Aircraft Corp. v. Rainey* (1988), another aspect of which is discussed in Chapter 10, provides a useful example. The case arose out of the fatal crash of a Navy airplane. The husband of one of the decedents, himself a Navy flight instructor, sued the manufacturer of the plane, and at trial, under questioning by the manufacturer, acknowledged that he had written a letter that contained some suggestions of pilot error. These were admissible as party admissions, and the trial court did not allow Rainey to introduce the portion of his letter concluding that a defect in the plane was the most probable primary cause of the accident. That was an abuse of discretion, the Supreme Court held, because it gave a distorted view of what Rainey had written.

4.   The "best evidence" rule and the demand for originals
      (FRE 1001–1008)

Geoffrey Gilbert, the first great treatise writer on Evidence in the English language, proclaimed that "[t]he first ... and most signal Rule" of Evidence is that a party must present "the best Evidence that the Nature of the Thing is capable of." (*The Law of Evidence* (1st ed. 1754), at pp. 3–4) Professor Nance has argued ably that the best-evidence rule remains a basic organizing principle of evidentiary law, but most modern analysts do not agree, and there is nothing in the FRE suggesting that it is. For the best-evidence principle to have force, a court would have to say, in effect, "Though that evidence is more probative than prejudicial, I'm going to exclude it because you could have presented better evidence." To be sure, there are outcroppings of such a principle in evidentiary law. The rule against hearsay may be considered one, so far as it applies to non-testimonial statements made by available declarants.

The rule against leading questions on direct appears to be another. But a court will not generally say something like, "That expert witness [or that statistical approach, or that question] is not bad, but you could have done better, so I'll sustain the objection." In general, a party is allowed to prove his case however he wants, as long as the probative value of the evidence is not outweighed by negative factors and the evidence does not run afoul of one of the prescribed exclusionary rules.

But there is one doctrine that sometimes still does go by the name of the "best evidence" rule. It applies only to a "writing, recording or photo-graph" (FRE 1002), a formulation that I shall replace with the shorthand *document*, and it provides as a presumptive matter that if you want to prove the contents of a document then you must present an original. As it is often said, the best evidence of the contents of a document is the document itself.

> Why "an" original rather than "the" original? Because there might be multiple originals. Suppose that at a closing, eight copies of a contract are signed, and each is intended to have the same effect. Each is considered an original. Or suppose information is electronically stored. An accurate printout or display of the information would be considered an original. (FRE 1001(d))

Now, one might say the same about almost anything; if we want to know what a car looked like, the best evidence would be the car itself. But the party is not required to bring in the car. He may instead present a witness who describes what the car looks like or a picture of the car. So why does a different rule apply to documents? Probably in part because they are easy to produce in court and requiring production might make fraud more difficult, and also in part because even an honest witness testifying from memory may fail to report accurately the contents of a document. Sometimes there are interesting questions of whether something should be deemed a document. For example, in one case a defendant charged with trafficking in counterfeit watches contended that the prosecution should have produced the watches as evidence, because the trademarks marked on them were part of what allegedly made them counterfeit. But the appellate court held that "[t]he viewing of a simple and recognized trademark is not likely to be inaccurately remembered," and while the trademark was *in* writing, it was more like a picture or symbol than a writing on a document; the watches could therefore be classified as chattels rather than as writings. (*United States v. Yasmin* (5th Cir. 1989))

It is important to recognize that the requirement for an original applies only if the proponent is attempting to prove the contents of the document as such – not if the proponent is attempting to prove a fact that a document could prove. Thus, if a witness testifies, "We did $800,000 in sales last April," the court would *not* say, "Disallowed. The better evidence would be the sales records." But if the proponent wants the witness to testify, "Our sales records show that we did $800,000 in sales record last year," the best-evidence rule would come into play and would presumptively bar the testimony, because it asserts not simply the underlying facts but *what the documents say.*

Bear in mind also that the best-evidence rule and the hearsay rule are very distinct. Thus, if a plaintiff wants to prove that the defendant made a fraudulent assertion in writing, the writing itself would be presumptively required, even though, far from being offered to prove the truth of what it asserts, it would be offered on the grounds that the assertion was false. Similarly, if a party wants to prove the terms of a written lease, the best-evidence rule would apply, even though those terms have no truth value.

I have spoken of the best-evidence rule as a presumptive requirement, because it does not exclude secondary evidence of the contents of the document if the proponent cannot feasibly produce any original. FRE 1004 lists situations in which production of an original is excused:

- All originals have been lost or destroyed, so long as this did not occur through bad faith conduct of the proponent; even if the proponent destroyed the only original, that would not be a problem if this occurred as part of a routine file clean-out before the litigation arose.
- The only original is in a third party's hands and the proponent cannot obtain it through judicial process.
- The original is in the hands of an adversary, who fails to produce it despite being on notice of the proponent's intention to prove its contents.
- The document "is not closely related to a controlling issue." This provision gives the court a bit of discretion to decline to enforce the rule if the costs of producing the original just don't seem worthwhile. And sometimes courts take into account not only the factors articulated by the Rule – how important the issue is to the case, and how closely related the document is – but also whether the contents of the document are sufficiently simple that there is little chance a witness would fail to describe them accurately. For example, in one case the evidence against the accused, Duffy, included testimony that a shirt bearing the laundry marking "D-U-F" was found in a stolen car. Upholding the conviction, the appellate court held that there was little danger that the witness would inaccurately remember the content of this simple inscription.

Other rules also provide mitigation in certain situations. FRE 1005 allows the contents of official records and those recorded or filed in public offices to be proven by a copy that has been certified in accordance with FRE 902 or that a witness can testify accurately reproduces the original. FRE 1006 allows a party to use "a summary, chart, or calculation" rather than voluminous documents, though the proponent must make the originals or duplicates available to other parties, and the court may still decide that those should be produced as evidence. And FRE 1007 relieves many party admissions from the exclusionary rule: A proponent may prove the contents of a document "by the testimony, deposition, or written statement" of the adverse party describing those contents.

> Recall that party admissions are relieved from the personal-knowledge and lay-opinion rules, as well as the hearsay rule. The rulemakers did not go quite so far in the present context: An oral admission, not made in a formal testimonial context, as to the contents of a document will not satisfy the best-evidence rule.

Plainly, best-evidence principles continue to play some role in crafting evidentiary rules. But, ironically, one may wonder whether in the context known as the best-evidence rule, the demand for documentary originals, the rule is worthwhile. A proponent usually has considerable incentive to produce an original, and if he does not it is easy enough for his opponent to point out the potential defects of the secondary evidence.

D. Preserving the record (FRE 103(a)–(c), (e))

If the court rules against you on an evidentiary matter, and you believe the ruling could (alone or in combination with others) lead to a reversal, you need to make your opposition apparent very promptly. (FRE 103(a)) If not, the appellate court is likely to say that review is foreclosed. This is a "fix it now" principle: The parties should give the trial court an opportunity to avoid a problem when that can be done relatively easily, rather than complain afterwards that a new trial is necessary. Note that this principle reflects the adversarial nature of the common-law system, which puts the primary responsibility for presenting a case, and even the initial responsibility for protecting their interests, on the parties themselves rather than on the court; thus, the court is not expected to know without being alerted why evidence should or should not be admitted. FRE 103(e) does articulate one limitation on this principle: if the trial error commits "a plain error affecting a substantial right," then the appellate court may remedy it. But that is a very hard standard to meet, and you never want to be in a position where you have to satisfy it.

So just what do you have to do to preserve the record? If your adversary offers evidence that you think should not be admitted, you should object. And if the evidence has come in before you could state your objection – it has been said that the chief hearsay exception is the quick answer – then you should move immediately to strike. Do you have to say anything beyond "Objection!" or "Move to strike"? That depends on what the court does. If the court sustains the objection or grants the motion to strike, then you've won this little battle and you needn't say, or have said, more. But if the court disagrees with you, then foggy brevity will not do. FRE 103(a)(1)(B) says an objection must state "the specific ground, unless it was apparent from the context." Appellate courts can be sticky on this. The basic lesson is that if you win with a vague objection, all well and good; but if you lose, you'd better be specific.

> If the court grants your motion to strike evidence that has already been heard, there's a question of what remedy is appropriate. The court should at least caution your adversary not to refer again to the struck evidence and instruct the jury to disregard it. In rare cases, a mistrial would be appropriate.

Now suppose you're trying to introduce evidence. Let's suppose, to start, that you ask a witness a question, your adversary says, "Objection. Hearsay," the court sustains the objection, and you believe that the ruling is erroneous and the harm potentially substantial. You must not only articulate *why* the court should admit the evidence but also make clear *what* the evidence is. Thus, FRE 103(a)(2) says you must inform the court of the substance of the evidence "by an offer of proof, unless the substance was apparent from the context." There are various methods of making an offer of proof. One is to summarize, on the record but outside the hearing of the jury, what you expect the witness would have answered. Or you may actually conduct the barred examination of the witness, again on the record but outside the jury's hearing; under FRE 103(c), the court may direct that you do it this way, which eliminates uncertainty as to what the testimony would have been but is more time-consuming. If, on the other hand, the evidence is a document rather than oral testimony, you can simply make sure that the document is made part of the record. In any event, you will want to eliminate doubt about what the evidence would have been so that the appellate court cannot cite such doubt to avoid review except under the plain-error standard.

In recent decades, one particular problem in preserving the record has become salient. Suppose you are representing a criminal defendant and contemplating putting him on the stand. But you may be hesitant, because your client has prior convictions (or a history of other acts that might be used to impeach his credibility if he testifies). So you ask the court to rule in advance whether the convictions would be admissible, and the court obliges: It holds that they would be. Recognizing that the impact of the convictions would likely be devastating, you decide to keep your client off the stand. He is convicted, and you appeal, contending that the trial court's ruling on the convictions was in error and that this deprived your client of the ability to testify in his own defense, which might have been crucial. But in *Luce v. United States* (1984), a decision followed by most states (but far from all), the U.S. Supreme Court held that the defendant can appeal on the basis of the ruling only if he decides to testify and the convictions are actually used against him. Among the reasons given by the *Luce* Court was that it was uncertain what the accused's testimony would have been; the Court thought an offer of proof would be unsatisfactory because the actual testimony might differ (though that would open the accused to devastating impeachment).

> *State v. Whitehead* (N.J. 1986) is a thoughtful state case rejecting *Luce*. Some, but not all, states declining to follow *Luce* require the accused to make an offer of proof.

Another reason was that the prosecutor might decide in the end not to use the convictions. How often does a prosecutor, having fought for and won the ability to use convictions for impeachment if the defendant testifies, decide not to bother when the defendant actually does take the stand? A few decades ago, I issued an invitation for anybody who is aware of such a case to tell me about it. Professor James Duane has repeated the invitation in front of large audiences of judges and criminal lawyers. We're still waiting, and the invitation is still open.

Meanwhile, the Supreme Court has made the situation even more difficult for criminal defendants. A defendant who decides to testify though he knows that prior convictions will be used against him often tries to "take the sting" out of the convictions by acknowledging them on direct and offering whatever expiation he can; this avoids the evasive appearance that can arise if the convictions are introduced on cross. But in *Ohler v. United States* (2000) the Supreme Court held that if he introduces the convictions himself, he cannot then appeal on the basis that they should not have been admitted. Some states follow *Ohler*, but a substantial number do not.

E. Judicial notice (FRE 201)

This section discusses three distinct concepts to which the term judicial notice is sometimes applied – fact-finder notice, judicial notice of adjudicative facts, and judicial notice of legislative facts.

Suppose that a driver is alleged to have been texting immediately before an accident. No evidence is necessary for the fact-finder to conclude that texting while driving is dangerous. That is the type of knowledge of the world that fact-finders, whether jurors or judges, are expected to bring with them into the courtroom. If the case is tried to a jury, we would not expect an instruction regarding this fact; the jury is free to act on the belief that it is true. This is sometimes called *jury notice*, though a more inclusive term would be *fact-finder notice*. If a judge is the fact-finder, she takes this type of notice in exercising that capacity, not as the officer presiding over the proceedings.

Now, to assess judicial notice proper, let's distinguish between two types of fact to which FRE 201 refers: *adjudicative* and *legislative* facts. An *adjudicative fact* is of significance to the particular case. It may arise in other cases, but it does not have any significance for determining law that transcends those cases. That US-23 is a highway running north and south along Ann Arbor, Michigan, is an adjudicative fact. FRE 201(b) prescribes circumstances in which a court can take notice of such a fact –

if it is "generally known within the trial court's territorial jurisdiction" or "can be accurately and readily determined from sources whose accuracy cannot reasonably be questioned." For a court sitting in Ann Arbor, the direction of US-23 could probably qualify on either ground; the fact is "generally known" in the jurisdiction, though presumably there are many people who have a weak sense of direction, and it could be readily determined from any reliable road atlas or online mapping service. A party may of course present reasons and evidence in an attempt to persuade the court not to take judicial notice of a fact, but once it is done the Rule contemplates that, at least in a civil case, no evidence on the point would be presented to the jury. In a civil case, the judge instructs the jurors that they must accept the fact as conclusively established. In a criminal case, in deference to the role of the jury, the Rule prescribes that the judge instructs the jurors that they *may* accept the fact; some common-law jurisdictions, though, would treat judicial notice as binding even against a criminal defendant.

FRE 201 explicitly does not cover what are known as *legislative facts*. The concept is an important one, but the term, coined by the great 20th-century scholar Kenneth Davis, is unfortunate, because ordinarily the legislature has nothing to do with these facts; to call them *lawmaking facts* would probably be more precise, because they are facts that help determine what the law is. For example, in *Brown v. Board of Education* (1954), the Supreme Court said that legal segregation of black schoolchildren from others "generates a feeling of inferiority as to their status in the community that may affect their hearts and minds in a way unlikely ever to be undone." Note that this is a factual assertion, not an assertion of law; but it is one that helps shape the law, and led to the conclusion that legal segregation in the public schools is unconstitutional. If the law is to be uniform across similar cases – and that seems to be virtually essential for it to be considered law – then facts of this sort must be determined uniformly across cases. And this means that a court is not bound by what is in the record or what the parties contend, and that an appellate court is not bound by what the trial court found – for if the appellate court had to defer, what would happen if different trial courts made contrary findings? Moreover, a court may make a finding of legislative fact (or act on an implicit understanding of one) even if, as in *Brown*, the fact appears disputable. The court has to decide what the law is, and if doing that depends on some understanding of a fact of the world, the court has to act on its understanding, no matter how contestable that may be.

At the same time, notice that the court may have control over the impact it accords to a particular factual proposition. In *Brown*, for example, the Court *could* have said, "*If* in a particular school district, segregation by law has an adverse impact on schoolchildren, then it is unconstitutional there." And if it had done so, the question of impact would have been an adjudicative fact, to be decided district by district. But that is not what the Court said (though initially some trial courts interpreted it that way). Instead, the Court enunciated a uniform nationwide rule that segregation by law in the public schools is unconstitutional, and that rule depended in part on a broad, transcendent perception of the impact of segregation on children.

I believe the concept of legislative facts is a powerful one, and is often misunderstood, or overlooked. Often, when a case involves a national issue of law, reviewing judges who approve of how the trial court came out on it will rely heavily on the trial court's findings of fact and complain about lack of deference by judges on the other side; but if those facts are used to determine what the law is and not matters of application in the particular case, then indeed there should be no deference, just as an appellate court does not defer to a trial court on a question of what the law is.

F. Burdens and presumptions (FRE 301)

We often speak of the burden of proof, but to be precise we should speak of two separate burdens, which usually run together, but not always – the burden of *persuasion* and the burden of *production*.

The *burden of persuasion* refers to how confident the fact-finder has to be at the end of the case to find for one side or the other. It depends on the relative weights that we attach to two types of error – finding for the defendant when the verdict should be against him, and finding against the defendant when the verdict should be for him. In a criminal case, the long-standing and well-justified view is that it is far worse to convict an innocent person than to acquit a guilty one. This leads to the standard, constitutionally required in the United States, of *proof beyond a reasonable doubt*. Efforts to quantify this burden seem inevitably to fail, but the essence of it is that the jury should not find against an accused unless it is virtually certain that he committed the crime charged, which requires a finding of near certainty on each element of the crime. Some common-law jurisdictions avoid this formulation altogether, and say more simply, but to similar effect, that the jury cannot convict unless it is sure of guilt.

In most civil cases, the received wisdom is that an error in favor of the defendant is about as bad as an error against him. And so the usual rule is that the plaintiff should win if the fact-finder concludes that the facts more likely than not support him – a standard (as noted on p. 148) that is most often enunciated in the United States with the unhelpful formula "preponderance of the evidence" and elsewhere by the more useful "balance of the probabilities."

> In some civil cases, such as for fraud, courts consciously apply a higher standard, often phrased as "clear and convincing evidence."

That the defendant wins in a state of absolute equipoise – where the facts as likely favor one side as the other – appears to be a mild reflection of the importance of inertia, the fact that a judgment against the defendant but not one against the plaintiff requires the imposition of judicial relief. I believe that inertia is probably more important than a mere tie-breaker. I suspect that, in deed though not in word, courts and juries implement a higher standard of persuasion. Such an elevated standard might help resolve some hypothetical conundrums, such as what should happen if the defendant is one of 1000 people who are equally likely to have been among the 501 gatecrashers at an event.

> Another puzzle, often called the problem of conjunction, has garnered much attention: Suppose a case has two elements, and the jury concludes that the first is true to a .6 probability, and that if the first is true the second is also true to a .6 probability. So the jury believes that each element is more likely than not true, but that it is only .36 probable that the facts favor the plaintiff. What should the jury do? I agree with Professor Nance that the difficulty dissolves if the court gives an aggregate instruction, telling the jurors that they can find for the plaintiff only if they conclude that the facts of the entire case, as well as on each element, favor the plaintiff.

Now, the court should not send a case to the jury unless it believes that the jury could reasonably find for either party; if it could reasonably find only for one party, then that party should be awarded judgment as a matter of law. (But not if that party is a prosecutor!) If neither side were to present any evidence at all, then the defendant, in either a criminal or a civil case, would be entitled to such a judgment. One way of expressing this is to say that the *burden of production* is on the prosecution or plaintiff, as the case may be. The burden on this party is to present enough evidence that the jury *could* reasonably find that it has met the burden of persuasion, so that judgment as a matter of law against it is not appropriate.

There are, however, some issues, called *affirmative defenses*, on which the burden of production is on the defendant. Examples include the insanity defense in a criminal case, contributory negligence in a civil case, and duress in either. Unless the defendant presents sufficient evidence of one of these, counsel cannot discuss the issue in closing argument and it will not be presented to the jury. The burden of persuasion on such a defense may go along with the burden of production, but not necessarily. Thus, some states impose on a criminal defendant not only the burden of producing evidence that he is insane but also the burden of persuasion, to various degrees. Others, and the federal jurisdiction, provide that if the defendant presents enough evidence of insanity the issue will go to the jury, and then it is the prosecution's burden to persuade the jury that the defendant was legally sane and so capable of committing the crime. That position may be required by the guarantee of the presumption of innocence in Article 6(2) of the ECHR, where it applies. (*R v. Lambert* (H.L. 2001))

One way of expressing the basic principle that the burden of production is on the prosecution on the elements of the crime is to say that the defendant is *presumed innocent*. In general terms, a presumption is a rule of law providing that on a given state of evidence a particular result is required. So the presumption of innocence means that if no evidence at all is presented, then judgment for the defendant follows. In general, presumptions follow this form: If the trier of fact finds predicate factual set A, then fact B is presumed, which means that the trier must find B to be true unless sufficient evidence of Not-B is presented, in which case the presumption effectively disappears. (The presumption of innocence can be thought of in these terms, with the predicate factual set A being the empty set, so that the presumption takes hold at the beginning of the case.)

Here are some typical presumptions:

- A letter properly stamped, addressed, and mailed will presumably reach its addressee.
- The driver of an automobile is presumed to have permission to drive it.
- If an automobile belongs to the driver's employer, the driver is presumed to be driving it on the employer's business.

Let's take the first of these – that a letter properly stamped, addressed, and mailed will reach its addressee. So the predicate fact A is that the letter is properly stamped, addressed, and mailed, and the presumed fact B is that it reaches its addressee. If the proponent presents enough evidence for the jury to find A, then the presumption comes into play. Assume to start that the opponent presents some evidence that the predicate A is not true, but no other evidence that the presumed fact B is not true. Then the court should instruct the jury that *if* it finds A to be true, then it *must* find B to be true. That is, if it finds the letter was properly stamped, addressed, and mailed, then it must find that the letter reached its addressee. And this instruction would usually be appropriate even if the opponent presented no evidence that the predicate A is false; the presumption compels a finding of the presumed fact only if the jury finds the predicate, and the jury is not compelled to do that, even if no evidence is presented against the predicate, unless the evidence favoring it is overwhelming. Note that there is no need to use the term presumption in instructing the jury; it is better to say simply, "If you find A then you must find B."

One way of thinking about a presumption is that it is a *conditional shift of the burden of production*. That is, *if* the jury finds the predicate fact A – that is the condition – then the proponent has not only *satisfied* the burden of production on the presumed fact B but *shifted* that burden to the opponent, so that if the opponent does not present sufficient evidence to support a finding of Not-B then the jury is compelled to find B. And what if the opponent *does* present sufficient evidence for the jury to find Not-B? Then the presumption has been *rebutted* and probably (one might say presumably) it effectively disappears. In most cases the evidence of the predicate A, if the jury believes it, is enough to support a finding of the presumed fact B, but no finding of B is compelled, even conditionally, because of the rebuttal evidence. So there is no need to give any instruction to the jury.

There is such a thing as an *irrebuttable presumption*, under which, if A is taken to be true, then B is deemed proven, and no amount of evidence of Not-B will change this result. So, rather than an evidentiary rule, this really amounts to a substantive rule that the legal consequences assigned to B will attach on a finding of A.

One other possible effect of the presumption remains: Some courts have held that a presumption in favor of a civil plaintiff shifts the burden of persuasion to the defendant. But in most cases this result would not be justified. There is nothing in most presumptions that alters the calculation of error costs that goes into the burden of persuasion. And so FRE 301, which provides rather cryptically that in a civil case "the party against whom a presumption is directed has the burden of producing evidence to rebut [it]," adds that the Rule leaves the burden of persuasion unmoved, "on the party who had it originally."

Rule 301 leaves criminal cases untouched, because of the constitutional implications of presumptions there. Legislatures often try to make prosecutions easier by providing in general terms that some predicate is sufficient for conviction. The Supreme Court previously created a good deal of confusion in this realm, in large part because of what Winston Churchill once called "terminological inexactitude" (House of Commons speech, February 22, 1906; quoted in *The Outlook*, February 24, 1906, at p. 250). Sometimes courts and legislatures have used the term presumption for a softer rule, that if the jury finds A then it *may* find B. Such a rule, really one creating a permissible *inference*, is constitutional if the connection between the predicate and inferred facts is strong enough, at least as applied to the particular case. Ultimately, the Court made clear that a "mandatory" presumption – what is referred to here and in the FRE as simply a presumption – applied in favor of the prosecution is unconstitutional because it would "require [the jury] to find the presumed fact if the State proves certain predicate facts," thus relieving the prosecution of its burden of proving all elements of the crime beyond a reasonable doubt. (*Carella v. California* (1989)) If the legislature had been so minded, it could have avoided the difficulty by altering the elements of the crime – providing, for example, that a person is guilty of embezzling a rental car if it is not returned within five days of the expiration of the rental agreement, rather than that embezzling is presumed in that circumstance. And it could have created such affirmative defenses as it thought necessary to prevent the definition of the crime from being too harsh. But such a recasting of the crime might not have expressed what the legislature regarded as wrongful about the conduct in question.

18 Closing reflections on evidence law

Having reached the end of this survey of the law of Evidence, I will not attempt to state any grand overarching thesis or summary of the field. You may have spotted some recurrent themes in this little book, such as the usefulness of the likelihood ratio as an analytical device and the repeated appearance of best-evidence considerations, but in my view they do not come close to providing organizing structure for the whole; there are just too many topics, of a highly varied nature, and too many considerations to package neatly.

I suppose if pressed to offer a general perspective I would draw on the insight of Thayer offered at the beginning of Chapter 2: Evidence that is not relevant to some material proposition, or has too little probative value, should not be admitted, but if the evidence does have substantial probative value then it ought to be admitted unless there is good reason not to. And a wide variety of reasons might counsel against or even preclude admission – most notably, saving time; preventing potential biasing effects; creating incentives for the presentation of better evidence and for beneficial out-of-court behavior; avoiding unnecessary and oppressive intrusions; and preserving the proper procedures for presentation of testimony. (I have discounted fear of overvaluation of evidence by the jury, because in most contexts I do not believe it well explains evidentiary rules.)

Taken together, these factors imply that Sir Rupert Cross's aim of abolishing the law of Evidence remains unattainable, and will do so for as long as we can foresee. And yet, I do believe that there has been incremental movement in that direction. Though I have not emphasized historical developments here except where I have thought it helpful for exposition of the current law of Evidence, it has struck me while writing the book how substantial the changes have been on many topics (not all) during my decades of observing and participating in the field. I believe that on the whole the changes have been, and will continue to be, in the direction of making the law less structured and more receptive to offered evidence.

That certainly has been the trend with respect to hearsay in much of the common-law world, and I expect the United States will follow; so long as the confrontation right is independently protected, that would be a highly desirable development.

One final thought: I have tried hard in this book to give an accurate account of the most important aspects of the black-letter law of Evidence as it prevails in the United States. So much of the substance of the book is the same as it would be if another American scholar had written it. But of course exposition of black-letter law has not been the limit of my aims. The choice of particular questions to emphasize and perspectives to offer, and for that matter the distribution of topics under-emphasized or over-looked completely, are all quite personal. The law of Evidence is complex and multi-faceted; others could take very different approaches with equal claims to validity. I only hope you find the one that I have taken here useful and interesting.

Bibliographical essay

The literature on Evidence law is vast, and I can hope in this brief essay only to point to a small selection of works (almost all of them American) that I believe might be useful; I could list far more works and still make many glaring omissions. Though I have leaned on the suggestions of colleagues in the Evidence community, other scholars would list a very different selection, in part because I will not hesitate to mention a healthy sample of my own works. One justification for that practice is that in the body of this book I have, for the most part, resisted the temptation to cite those works; another is that in those works readers can find further elaboration of the perspectives presented in this book.

Let's begin with treatises. John Henry Wigmore's monumental treatise is still useful, though largely for historical purposes; the third edition was revised by James Chadbourn and Peter Tillers. A successor treatise, *The New Wigmore*, is in preparation under my general editorship, and several volumes, by an array of authors, are available, along with supplements. *Weinstein's Federal Evidence*, now curated by Mark S. Brodin, is a very useful work focused on the Federal Rules of Evidence (FRE); Jack B. Weinstein, the original author, was a member of the initial Advisory Committee that produced the FRE. Another helpful multi-volume treatise with a similar focus is the Evidence unit of Charles Alan Wright's *Federal Practice and Procedure*, with volumes by Kenneth W. Graham, Jr., Victor J. Gold, Jeffrey Bellin, and Daniel D. Blinka.

Among one-volume treatments, I will mention just a few. *Cross and Tapper on Evidence*, now edited by Roderick Munday and in its 13th edition, is a classic work for English law, with some attention to other common-law jurisdictions. *McCormick on Evidence*, now under the general editorship of Robert P. Mosteller and in its eighth edition (also available in a two-volume practitioner edition), is the best-established American work. *Evidence*, by Christopher B. Mueller, Laird C. Kirkpatrick, and Liesa Richter, now in its sixth edition, is another leading work, focused on the FRE. I will also mention a textbook of mine, *The Elements of Evidence* (5th ed. 2023), not because it has achieved anything like the prominence of the others but because it lays out more fully many of the thoughts summarized in this book.

Monographs of interest include: Edmund Morris Morgan, *Some Problems of Proof Under the Anglo-American System of Litigation* (1956); L. Jonathan Cohen, *The Probable and the Provable* (1977); William Twining, *Theories of Evidence: Bentham and Wigmore* (1985) (and note also his *Rethinking Evidence: Exploratory Essays* (2nd ed. 2006)); Barbara J. Shapiro, *Beyond Reasonable Doubt and Probable Cause: Historical Perspectives on the Anglo-American Law of Evidence* (1991); Mirjan Damaška, *Evidence Law Adrift* (1997); and Dale A. Nance, *Burdens of Proof: Discriminatory Power, Weight of Evidence, and Tenacity of Belief* (2016).

Some classic articles from the first half of the 20th century are: John MacArthur Maguire, *The Hillmon Case – Thirty-three Years After*, 38 Harv. L. Rev. 709 (1925); John MacArthur Maguire and Charles S.S. Epstein, *Preliminary Questions of Fact in Determining the Admissibility of Evidence*, 40 Harv. L. Rev. 392 (1927); Robert M. Hutchins and Donald Slesinger, *Some Observations on the Law of Evidence*, 28 Colum. L. Rev. 432 (1928); and Edmund M. Morgan, *The Hearsay Rule*, 12 Wash. L. Rev. 1 (1937).

Among the works that, in the middle of the second half of the 20th century, generated considerable debate concerning fundamental issues of proof, in addition to that of L. Jonathan Cohen, are: John Kaplan, *Decision Theory and the Factfinding Process*, 20 Stan. L. Rev. 1065 (1968); Richard O. Lempert, *Modeling Relevance*, 75 Mich. L. Rev. 1021 (1977); and Laurence H. Tribe, *Trial by Mathematics: Precision and Ritual in the Legal Process*, 84 Harv. L. Rev. 1329 (1971). At least four symposia (the first two organized by the late Peter Tillers) have included extensive discussion of the appropriateness of using conventional probability theory to model the fact-finding process. *Probability and Inference in the Law of Evidence*, 66 B.U. L. Rev. 377 (1986); *Decision and Inference in Litigation*, 13 Cardozo L. Rev. 253 (1991); *Bayesianism and Juridical Proof*, 1 Intl J. of Evidence & Proof 253 (1997); and *New Perspectives on Evidence*, 87 Va. L. Rev. 1491

(2001). Note also the more informal discussion in Ronald J. Allen, et al., *Probability and Proof in State v. Skipper: An Internet Exchange*, Jurimetrics 35, no. 3 (1995): 277, 285. Much of the discussion in these sources concerns problems of relevance and probative value. On conditional relevance, see Ronald J. Allen, *The Myth of Conditional Relevancy*, 25 Loy. L.A. L. Rev. 871 (1992); Richard D. Friedman, *Conditional Probative Value: Neoclassicism Without Myth*, 93 Mich. L. Rev. 439 (1994); and the subsequent exchange in volumes 93 and 94 of the *Michigan Law Review*, with pieces by Peter Tillers, Dale Nance, and myself.

Three influential articles on the history of evidence law are John H. Langbein, *Historical Foundations of the Law of Evidence: A View from the Ryder Sources, 96 Colum. L. Rev. 1168* (1996); T.P. Gallanis, *The Rise of Modern Evidence Law*, 84 Iowa L. Rev. 499 (1999); and Eleanor Swift, *One Hundred Years of Evidence Law Reform: Thayer's Triumph*, 88 Cal. L. Rev. 2437 (2000).

On the theoretical underpinnings of the testimonial approach to confrontation, see my essay *Confrontation: The Search for Basic Principles*, 86 Georgetown L.J. 1011 (1998); and an article co-authored with Bridget McCormack, *Dial-In Testimony*, 150 U. Pa. L. Rev. 1171 (2002). A range of academic responses to adoption of the testimonial approach presented in *Crawford v. Washington* is presented in a symposium organized by Robert Pitler, Crawford *and Beyond: Exploring the Future of the Confrontation Clause in Light of its Past*, in volume 71 of the *Brooklyn Law Review* (2005). I have written a great deal on forfeiture of the confrontation right, including *Confrontation and the Definition of Chutzpa*, 31 Israel L. Rev. 506 (1997); and *Giles v. California: A Personal Reflection*, 13 Lewis & Clark L. Rev. 733 (2009). Other articles in a symposium presented in that volume of the *Lewis & Clark Law Review* offer a variety of views. I comment on significant developments in the law of confrontation on the Confrontation Blog, www.confrontationright.blogspot.com.

In addition to those already listed, I will mention only a relatively few pieces on hearsay. Many people find Laurence H. Tribe, *Triangulating Hearsay*, 87 Harv. L. Rev. 957 (1974) helpful in understanding what statements are hearsay. I offer a more elaborate diagrammatic approach, one with broader applications and ties to Bayesian probability, in *Route Analysis of Credibility and Hearsay*, 96 Yale L.J. 667 (1987). I have found the analysis in Roger C. Park, *McCormack on Hearsay and the Concept of*

Hearsay: A Critical Analysis Followed by Suggestions to Law Teachers, 65 Minn. L. Rev. 423 (1980), to be extremely insightful. An array of views on so-called implied assertions may be found in *Symposium on Hearsay and Implied Assertions: How Would (or Should) the Supreme Court Decide the Kearley Case?*, 16 Miss. Coll. L. Rev. 1 (1995), organized by Craig Callen. On prior statements of an in-court witness, see my *Prior Statements of a Witness: A Nettlesome Corner of the Hearsay Thicket*, 1995 S.Ct. Rev. 277. And on excited utterances, the following exchange, though pre-*Crawford*, remains of interest: Aviva Orenstein, *"MY GOD!": A Feminist Critique of the Excited Utterance Exception to the Hearsay Rule*, 85 CAL. L. Rev. 159, 211 (1996); Randolph N. Jonakait, *MY GOD! Is this How a Feminist Analyzes Excited Utterances?*, 4 Wm. & M. J. of Women & the Law 263 (1997); and Aviva Orenstein, *Evidence in a Different Voice: Some Thoughts on Professor Jonakait's Critique of a Feminist Approach*, 4 Wm. & M. J. of Women & the Law 295 (1997).

Here is a short selection of works bearing on issues relating to witnesses. Cheryl Hanna, *No Right to Choose: Mandated Victim Participation in Domestic Violence Prosecutions*, 109 Harv. L. Rev. 1849 (1996), argues ably for the position suggested by the title. Mark Spottswood, *Live Hearings and Paper Trials*, 38 Fl. St. U. L. Rev. 827 (2011), examines the limited ability of jurors to assess credibility based on witness demeanor. My article, *Character Impeachment: Psycho-Baysesian (!?) Analysis and a Proposed Overhaul*, 38 UCLA L. Rev. 637 (1991), presents an extended argument in favor of the view presented in this book that character impeachment evidence of a criminal defendant ought not to be allowed. With respect to child witnesses, a good place to start is the treatise by John E.B. Myers, which now goes by the title *Evidence of Interpersonal Violence: Child Maltreatment, Intimate Partner Violence, Rape, Stalking, and Elder Abuse*. On research findings regarding children and their applicability to the real world, see this exchange: Thomas D. Lyon, *The New Wave in Children's Suggestibility Research: A Critique*, 84 Cornell L. Rev. 1004 (1999); Stephen J. Ceci and Richard D. Friedman, *The Suggestibility of Children: Scientific Research and Legal Implications*, 86 Cornell L. Rev. 1 (2000); Thomas D. Lyon, *Applying Suggestibility Research to the Real World: the Case of Repeated Questions*, 65 Law & Contemp. Probs. 97 (2002).

Aviva Orenstein, *No Bad Men!: A Feminist Analysis of Character Evidence in Rape Trials*, 49 Hastings L.J. 663 (1998), argues from a feminist perspective against rules allowing evidence of prior sexual misconduct of an accused, and in favor of an expanded role for expert evidence to educate the jury about rape. For a nuanced analysis (somewhat at variance from my own) of issues surrounding rape-shield laws, see Deborah Tuerkheimer, *Judging Sex*, 97 Cornell L. Rev. 1461 (2012). And for a broader presentation of a feminist perspective on Evidence law, see especially Kit Kinports, *Evidence Engendered*, 1991 U. Ill. L. Rev. 413 (1991).

On scientific evidence, a useful exploration of some of the issues that led the *Daubert* Court to adopt a system of reliability testing is Paul C. Giannelli, *The Admissibility of Novel Scientific Evidence: Frye v. United States, a Half-Century Later*, 80 Colum. L. Rev. 1197 (1980). For thorough explorations of the particular dispute underlying *Daubert*, see Joseph Sanders, *Bendectin on Trial* (1998), and Michael D. Green, *Bendectin and Birth Defects* (1996). David E. Bernstein, *The Misbegotten Judicial Resistance to the* Daubert *Revolution*, 89 N.D. L. Rev. 27 (2013), reviews developments both before and after *Daubert* and defends the transformation it wrought. Among the many significant contributions of David Kaye are *The Double Helix and the Law of Evidence* (2010); *The Probability of an Ultimate Issue: The Strange Cases of Paternity Testing*, 75 Iowa L. Rev. 75 (1989); *Is Proof of Statistical Significance Relevant?*, 61 Wash. L. Rev. 1333 (1986); and *The Limits of the Preponderance of the Evidence Standard: Justifiable Naked Statistical Evidence and Multiple Causation*, 7 Am. Bar Found. Res. J. 487 (1982). Jonathan J. Koehler has written several excellent pieces on the particular problem of presentation of DNA evidence, including *The Psychology of Numbers in the Courtroom: How to Make DNA-Match Statistics Seem Impressive or Insufficient*, 74 S. Cal. L. Rev. 1275 (2001).

For an informed and perceptive understanding of the law of evidentiary privilege and the empirical assumptions underlying it, see Edward J. Imwinkelried, *Questioning the Behavioral Assumption Underlying Wigmorean Absolutism in the Law of Evidentiary Privileges*, 65 U. Pitt. L. Rev. 145 (2004).

On judicial notice, see Kenneth Culp Davis, *Judicial Notice*, 55 Colum. L. Rev. 945 (1955), elaborating on the fundamental distinction between legislative and adjudicative fact that he had previously highlighted. Dale A. Nance, *The Best Evidence Principle*, 73 Iowa L. Rev. 227 (1988), is a landmark article arguing that the best-evidence principle is far more important than has been recognized in recent decades. Nance has also written two important articles on completeness, *A Theory of Verbal Completeness*, 80 Iowa L. Rev. 825 (1995), and *Verbal Completeness and Exclusionary Rules Under the Federal Rules of Evidence*, 75 Tex. L. Rev. 51 (1996).

Finally, matters of race are often present, explicitly or not, in evidentiary issues. Three significant articles discussing, among other issues, the problem of how to deal with biases based on stereotypes and "unscreened evidence" are I. Bennett Capers, *Evidence Without Rules*, 94 N.D. L. Rev. 867 (2018); Mikah Thompson, *Bias on Trial: Toward an Open Discussion of Racial Stereotypes in the Courtroom*, 2018 Mich. St. L. Rev. 1243 (2018); and Montré Carodine, *Contemporary Issues in Critical Race Theory: Race as Character Evidence in High Profile Cases*, 75 U. Pitt. L. Rev. 679 (2014). Joseph W. Rand, *The Demeanor Gap: Race, Lie Detection, and the Jury*, 33 Conn. L. Rev. 1 (2000), discusses the difficulties that jurors tend to have in assessing credibility of witnesses of another race. Among the issues discussed in Jasmine B. Gonzales Rose, *Toward a Critical Race Theory of Evidence*, 101 Minn. L. Rev. 2243, 2279 (2017), is the bearing of race on evidence of flight by the accused. And Gabriel J. Chin, *"A Chinaman's Chance" in Court: Asian Pacific Americans and Racial Rules of Evidence*, 3 U.C. Irvine L. Rev. 965 (2013), discusses racially based presumptions that applied against persons of Chinese ancestry.

Index

Titles in the **Elgar Advanced Introductions** series include:

International Political Economy
Benjamin J. Cohen

The Austrian School of Economics
Randall G. Holcombe

Cultural Economics
Ruth Towse

Law and Development
Michael J. Trebilcock and Mariana Mota Prado

International Humanitarian Law
Robert Kolb

International Trade Law
Michael J. Trebilcock

Post Keynesian Economics
J.E. King

International Intellectual Property
Susy Frankel and Daniel J. Gervais

Public Management and Administration
Christopher Pollitt

Organised Crime
Leslie Holmes

Nationalism
Liah Greenfeld

Social Policy
Daniel Béland and Rianne Mahon

Globalisation
Jonathan Michie

Entrepreneurial Finance
Hans Landström

International Conflict and Security Law
Nigel D. White

Comparative Constitutional Law
Mark Tushnet

International Human Rights Law
Dinah L. Shelton

Entrepreneurship
Robert D. Hisrich

International Tax Law
Reuven S. Avi-Yonah

Public Policy
B. Guy Peters

The Law of International Organizations
Jan Klabbers

International Environmental Law
Ellen Hey

International Sales Law
Clayton P. Gillette

Corporate Venturing
Robert D. Hisrich

Public Choice
Randall G. Holcombe

Private Law
Jan M. Smits

Consumer Behavior Analysis
Gordon Foxall

Behavioral Economics
John F. Tomer

ELGAR ADVANCED INTRODUCTIONS: LAW

www.advancedintros.com

Access the whole eBook collection at a cost effective price for law students at your institution.

Email: **sales@e-elgar.co.uk** for more information